Training for
SOCCER PLAYERS

Marc Briggs

THE CROWOOD PRESS

First published in 2013 by
The Crowood Press Ltd
Ramsbury, Marlborough
Wiltshire SN8 2HR

www.crowood.com

British Library Cataloguing-in-Publication Data
A catalogue record for this book is available from the British Library.

ISBN 978 1 84797 477 8

All diagrams by Charlotte Kelly, except Fig. 9 by Keith Field.

Acknowledgements
Kelvin Beeching wrote chapters 4, 5 and 6 of this book. Kelvin is a lecturer in Performance Analysis and Sport Coaching at the University of Worcester. He has a range of coaching experience from working in both participation and performance levels of sport in both football and cricket. He has experience of both coaching and sport science support in a professional setting, working with a range of athletes from footballers to ice hockey players.
Russell Warren wrote Chapter 8. Russell has worked as a graduate tutor in Sports Coaching at Northumbria University and has an MSc in Sport Coaching. He has a diverse coaching background and has coached football extensively, working with both the academy and first team at Falkirk FC, as well as a range of clubs in the north-east of England.

Typeset by Jean Cussons Typesetting, Diss, Norfolk

Printed and bound in India by Replika Press Pvt Ltd

CONTENTS

INTRODUCTION

Soccer is one the world's most popular forms of sport, being played in every nation, from grassroots to élite level. Training for soccer, for all abilities, is therefore an essential area, and one which has seen a significant amount of development over recent years. Soccer training can be adapted to meet the demands of players of all abilities, whether their goal is to improve their general fitness so they can enjoy the game at a recreational level, or to succeed at the highest level. Regardless of individual circumstances, all training programmes should be underpinned by a strategic theoretical framework with an understanding and appreciation of how the body functions in order for the training to have effective adaptations. Furthermore, training needs to be structured to coincide with the physiological demands associated with soccer, to ensure that training programmes are relevant and specific to the context of soccer, which will allow greater improvements in performance.

It is imperative that all practitioners are aware of soccer training principles so they can incorporate an effective intervention when necessary to suit the individual needs of the player. There is no universal 'magic' formula for enhancing performance; however, acquiring knowledge in relation to the adaptation process associated with the various forms of training is an essential prerequisite to developing effective training programmes that ultimately will improve soccer performance.

This book outlines the functions and mechanics of the human body, and how this directly relates to the physical demands of soccer. Specific training methodology will also be addressed in relation to aerobic and anaerobic training. The principles of programme design will be discussed, as well as guidelines on designing a training programme for all abilities. Means of fitness testing will also be investigated to ensure that practitioners can monitor and evaluate training programmes. Finally, effective nutritional strategies will be outlined, as this is an essential area that can influence the ability of athletes to train and perform.

CHAPTER 1

THE MECHANICS OF THE HUMAN BODY

Although it may not be necessary for a soccer player or coach to possess a comprehensive knowledge of sport and exercise physiology, it is, however, important to understand the basic principles in order to fully appreciate why certain training programmes are prescribed, and the need to incorporate a structured approach to programme design. Understanding the mechanics of the human body will enable the coach to devise individual training programmes for him or herself or the players he or she coaches, which will ultimately reduce the risk of injury and maximize performance benefits. This chapter will investigate the function of the human body in relation to bones, joints and muscles, as well as providing an overview of the energy systems the body utilizes during soccer performance.

The Human Skeleton

The human skeleton is comprised of 206 bones, which serve as a framework for the body. Once it is fully developed, the adult skeleton equates to approximately 30 to 40 per cent of the total bodyweight. Although the skeleton is imperative to everyday life, it does not work in isolation and is supported and supplemented by muscles, ligaments, tendons and cartilage. It is important to understand the function and structure of the skeleton in

relation to developing technique and fitness in a training programme, especially when working with young athletes, and athletes returning to training after suffering serious injury to bones.

The skeleton has five basic functions: support, protection, movement, the production of blood cells, and the storage of minerals.

Support: The skeleton is the body's framework and supports softer tissues as well as providing points of attachments for the majority of skeletal muscle.

Protection: The framework of the skeleton provides protection for many of the body's internal organs, to prevent injury to these. For example the ribs or thorax protect the heart and lungs.

Movement: The bones, joints and skeletal muscles work in partnership to enable the body to move effectively when the associated skeletal muscles contract. This allows different parts of the body to operate in the necessary precise movement patterns associated with soccer performance.

The production of blood cells: The red bone marrow contained within some of the larger bones produces red blood cells, which are responsible for the transport of oxygen

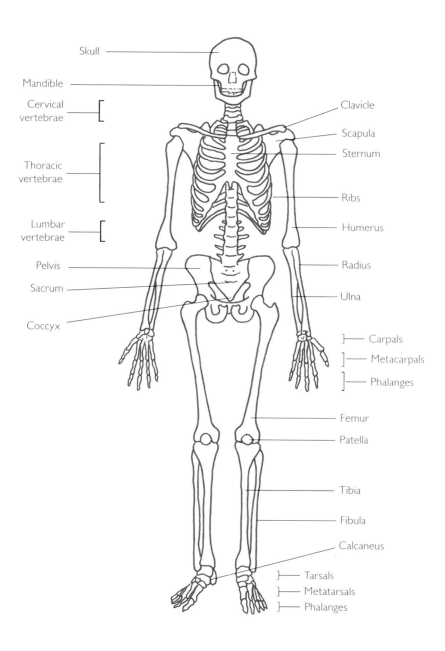

Fig. 1   The human skeleton.

around the body. The red bone marrow also produces white blood cells, which are integral to the body's immune system and defence against infection.

The storage of minerals: Bones can store several minerals, most importantly calcium and phosphorous. When the body detects a deficiency in these minerals, bones release these minerals into the blood to rectify the imbalance. However, it is important not to become over-reliant on this source, as calcium taken from the bones can result in their becoming more brittle.

Types of Bones

Bones are classified into five different types, usually according to their shape – long, short, flat, irregular and sesamoid.

Long bones: These are the larger bones of the body, such as the femur, humerus and tibia: they act as effective levers for movement.

Short bones: These are small bones but they are extremely strong, providing support and stability with little movement. They are well adapted to resist compression forces. Examples include the carpals and tarsals.

Flat bones: These are strong, flat plates of bone, their major function being the protection of vital organs. Flat bones are often fused together by cartilage for additional strength – for example the skull and the ribs. When fully formed in adulthood, flat bones are predominantly responsible for the production of red blood cells.

Irregular bones: These bones are categorized as irregular due to their non-uniform shape. Examples of irregular bones include the vertebrae, the sacrum and the mandible.

Sesamoid bones: These are usually small, oval-shaped bones embedded in a tendon. They are generally located in areas of intense pressure, the most common example being the patella (knee cap). Sesamoid bones are usually present in tendons which pass over a joint, to provide protection to the tendon.

Figure 1 demonstrates where the various types of bone are located within the human body, and shows clearly that the human skeleton is comprised of a complex collection of bones, all having a specific role to play.

Training Effects on Bones

Once the function and structure of the skeleton is fully understood, it is important to apply this knowledge to soccer training and performance. Regular training is crucial for increasing bone width and density, and also for the stimulation of bone tissue, as this must increase in order to compensate for the stresses placed on the bones during training. However, it is essential to ensure that the regular training is of optimal intensity: if the training is too intense it can cause injury and damage to bone, and conversely, insufficient stress on bone tissue can result in atrophy, meaning a reduction in the weight and strength of the bone, which can also be problematic. For example, if a player is training and competing regularly and suffers a long-term injury, then it is important to increase the training intensity gradually once he is fully fit to allow his bones to adapt back to the previous training intensity. Bones are the slowest of all tissues to recover, therefore progress should be carefully considered when getting a player back into full training following an injury.

Bones change shape and size during spells of growth and development, therefore a training programme needs to be appropriate for young athletes in order to protect the growth plates in the skeleton against potential damage. The injury known as 'Osgood Schlatter's condition' is quite common in the adolescent soccer player, and is caused by stress on the patella tendon that attaches the quadriceps muscles at the front of the thigh to the tibial tuberosity. This could be attributed to a training programme that is too intense for the adolescent player. Training programmes need to be modified for adolescent players, especially during times of growth and development.

Joints

Acquiring a wider knowledge of the various joints of the human body will enable a player or coach to prescribe training methods that improve technique and develop flexibility, both of which will help in the prevention of injury. The full range of joints in the player's body is needed in order to perform all the complex movement patterns associated with sports performance. Joints are broadly categorized into three different types according to their range of movement, namely fibrous, cartilaginous and synovial. *Fibrous* joints are strong and immovable, such as the joints between the bones of the skull. *Cartilaginous* joints allow only slight movement, for example the joints in the spine. *Synovial* joints are free-moving joints that are responsible for the movement patterns associated with soccer performance; they are characterized by the presence of synovial fluid in the space that encapsulates the articulating surfaces. They can be broken down further into six categories: ball and socket, hinge, pivot, condyloid, gliding and saddle joints.

Ball and socket: This joint allows the widest range of movement, enabling bending in several directions, creating a highly stable,

strong joint. Examples include the shoulder and hip joints.

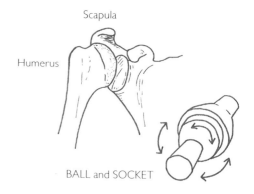

Fig. 2   Ball and socket joint.

Hinge: This joint allows for stable flexion and extension, permitting movement in only one plane. Examples include the knee, elbow and fingers.

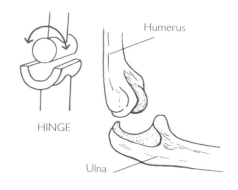

Fig. 3   Hinge joint.

Pivot: This joint allows rotational movement, enabling a turning motion without sideways displacement or bending. Examples include the axis and atlas vertebrae of the neck.

Gliding joint: This small joint allows for smooth movement along a plane or other smooth surface, the direction depending on the shape of the joint surface. Examples include the carpal bones of the feet and hands.

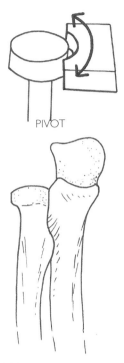

PIVOT

Fig. 4   Pivot joint.

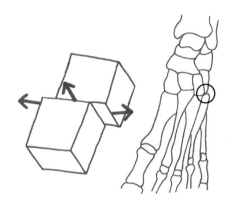

Fig. 6   Gliding joint.

Saddle joint: These joints permit move-ment in two planes at right angles to each other, which allows bending motion in several directions; an example is the base of the thumb.

Condyloid joint: These joints are slightly different, having irregular surfaces in which bones move past one another. The radio-carpal joint of the wrist is one example.

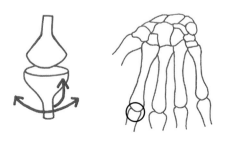

Fig. 5   Condyloid joint.

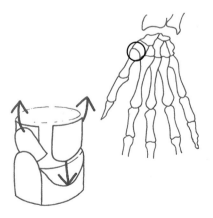

Fig. 7   Saddle joint.

11

Classification of Movements

Flexion	Movement that decreases the angle at a joint, usually bending a limb
Extension	Movement that increases the angle at a joint, usually straightening a limb
Abduction	Movement of a limb away from the midline of the body
Adduction	Movement of a limb towards the midline of the body
Internal rotation	Circular movement of a limb towards the body
External rotation	Circular movement of a limb away from the body
Circumduction	Movement of a limb in a circular or cone-shaped path
Plantar flexion	Movement extending the foot away from the body
Dorsiflexion	Movement pulling the foot up towards the shin
Inversion	Turning the sole of the foot inwards to face towards the midline
Eversion	Turning the sole of the foot outwards to face away from the midline
Supination	Complex movement of the hand to face palm upwards
Pronation	Complex movement of the hand to face palm downwards

Types of Movement

Once the different types of joint in the body are also fully understood it is important to appreciate the different types of movement they can produce, as each joint has its own range and type of movement. The table 'Classification of Movements' highlights the different movements that occur at synovial joints in the body.

All movements are described in relation to the anatomical position, generally as moving away from or towards it. It is therefore important to appreciate that most movements have an accompanying movement in the opposite direction. Figure 8 demonstrates some of the movements most prevalent in soccer.

Muscles

So far we have looked at the role of the skeleton and joints in the human body. However, without muscles, no movement would occur. Muscles are essential components of our body, with considerable demands placed on them. There are three types of muscle in the body:

cardiac, smooth and skeletal. *Cardiac* muscle is highly specialized and is only found in the heart. *Smooth* muscle is located in the digestive tract and in the circulatory and respiratory systems, and functions involuntarily. Although these two types of muscle are important to the human body, the main type of muscle in relation to movement is *skeletal* muscle. Skeletal muscle is designed for contraction and can be controlled voluntarily; it can also have a fast involuntary contraction such as a reflex response. All the major skeletal muscles in the human body are identified in Figure 9.

The Structure of Skeletal Muscle

The human body has over 600 skeletal muscles, which are responsible for exerting the force that creates most of the movement required for soccer. It is important for players and coaches to understand the structure of the skeletal muscles to ensure that throughout training, techniques are developed that are both effective and safe, as well as ultimately optimising strength.

Skeletal muscle is composed of *contractile tissue* that enables the muscle to contract, as

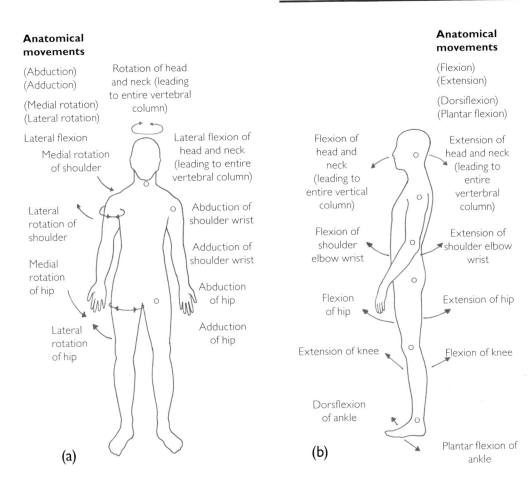

Anatomical movements

(Abduction)
(Adduction)

(Medial rotation)
(Lateral rotation)

Lateral flexion

Medial rotation of shoulder

Lateral rotation of shoulder

Medial rotation of hip

Lateral rotation of hip

Rotation of head and neck (leading to entire vertebral column)

Lateral flexion of head and neck (leading to entire vertebral column)

Abduction of shoulder wrist

Adduction of shoulder wrist

Abduction of hip

Adduction of hip

(a)

Anatomical movements

(Flexion)
(Extension)

(Dorsiflexion)
(Plantar flexion)

Flexion of head and neck (leading to entire vertical column)

Flexion of shoulder elbow wrist

Flexion of hip

Extension of knee

Dorsflexion of ankle

Extension of head and neck (leading to entire verterbral column)

Extension of shoulder elbow wrist

Extension of hip

Flexion of knee

Plantar flexion of ankle

(b)

Fig. 8   Anatomical movements of the synovial joints.

well as *connective tissue* that binds the muscle together. The muscle also contains nerves, which allow messages to be sent from the brain and spinal cord to the muscle via the central nervous system. *Blood vessels* are also found in the muscle: these transport oxygen, supply energy and maintain fluid levels, as well as removing waste products.

Muscle-Fibre Types

Each muscle contains many thousands of muscle fibres, however not all have the same characteristics. There are both genetic and training determinants of the type and quality of an individual's muscle-fibre composition: the specific muscle-fibre type and quality is genetically determined, but the actual size and metabolic capacity of the muscle can be improved with training.

Generally, there are three main types of skeletal muscle fibre: Type I, Type IIa and Type IIb.

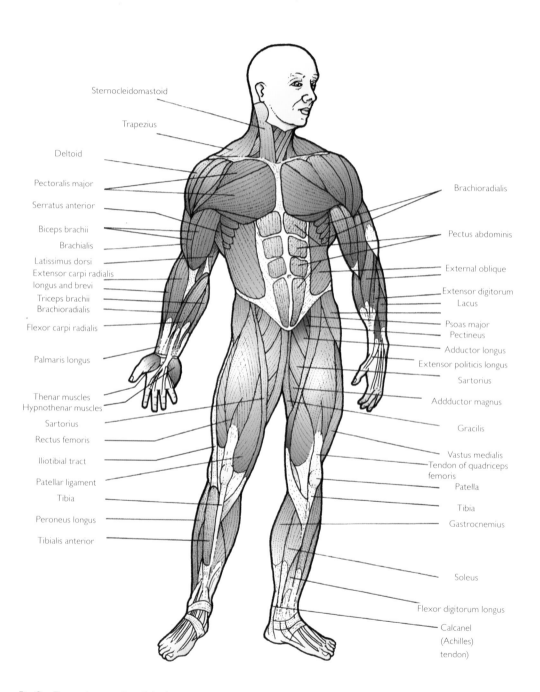

Sternocleidomastoid

Trapezius

Deltoid

Pectoralis major

Serratus anterior

Biceps brachii
Brachialis
Latissimus dorsi
Extensor carpi radialis
longus and brevi
Triceps brachii
Brachioradialis
Flexor carpi radialis

Palmaris longus

Thenar muscles
Hypnothenar muscles
Sartorius
Rectus femoris

Iliotibial tract

Patellar ligament
Tibia

Peroneus longus

Tibialis anterior

Brachioradialis

Pectus abdominis

External oblique

Extensor digitorum
Lacus

Psoas major
Pectineus

Adductor longus

Extensor politicis longus

Sartorius

Addductor magnus

Gracilis

Vastus medialis
Tendon of quadriceps
femoris
Patella

Tibia

Gastrocnemius

Soleus

Flexor digitorum longus

Calcanel
(Achilles)
tendon)

Fig. 9   The major muscles of the human body.

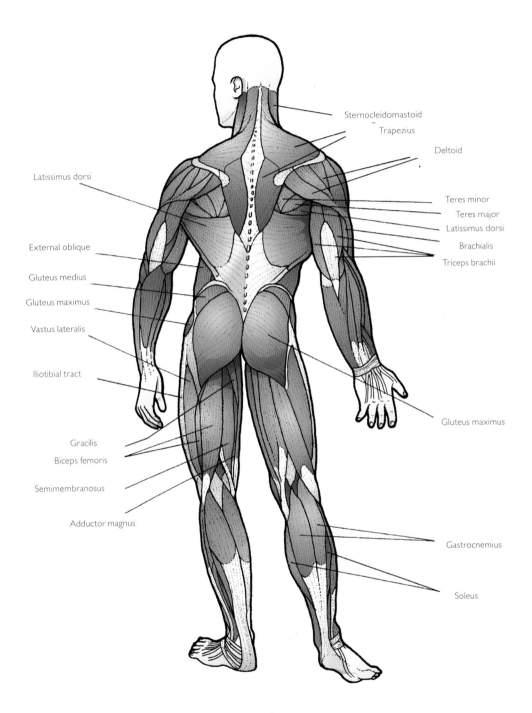

Sternocleidomastoid

Trapezius

Deltoid

Latissimus dorsi

Teres minor

Teres major

Latissimus dorsi

Brachialis

Triceps brachii

External oblique

Gluteus medius

Gluteus maximus

Vastus lateralis

Iliotibial tract

Gluteus maximus

Gracilis

Biceps femoris

Semimembranosus

Adductor magnus

Gastrocnemius

Soleus

Fig. 9   The major muscles of the human body continued.

Type I fibres: More commonly known as 'slow-twitch' fibres, these are characterized by their ability to contract and relax slowly, as well as by their resistance to fatigue. This makes them ideal for aerobic endurance activities such as long distance running, cycling or swimming.

Type IIa fibres: More commonly known as 'fast-twitch' fibres, these have the unique capability of working both aerobically and anaerobically. They possess less aerobic capability than the slow-twitch fibres, but more than Type IIb fibres. Type IIa fibres can change their characteristics in response to different training programmes, adapting to the specificity of the training demands.

Type IIb fibres: Similar to Type IIa fibres, these are also regarded as 'fast-twitch' fibres. Type IIb fibres are capable of contracting twice as fast as slow-twitch fibres, producing very high forces of short duration; however, they tend to fatigue quickly. Type IIb fibres only have the capability for anaerobic work, making them ideal for sprint-based activities. For example, top class sprinters will have a high proportion of this type of fibre.

It is important to take into account that certain players may be more suited to certain positions in a game of soccer as a result of their muscle-fibre make-up. Although the metabolic capacity and efficiency of the muscle fibre can be enhanced through training, ultimately the proportion of each muscle fibre is genetically predetermined. For example, a player with a higher proportion of fast-twitch fibres may be more effective as an attacker because he has a higher speed to get past defenders. However, there are obviously more variables than muscle-fibre proportion which need to be considered when selecting a team or when opting to play in a certain position. Nevertheless, it is beneficial for a coach or player to have an understanding of certain factors that may limit an individual's capability when training and competing.

Types of Muscle Action

There are three types of muscle action: isotonic, isometric and isokinetic.

Isotonic: This type of contraction causes the muscle to change length as it contracts, therefore resulting in the movement of a body part. This is the most common type of contraction, and is further classified into *concentric action* and *eccentric action*:

- *Concentric action* causes the muscle to shorten and thicken as it contracts. For example, doing a bicep curl – bending the elbow from straight to fully flexed – causes a concentric contraction of the bicep muscle. Concentric contractions are the most common type of muscle contraction and are evident in all sporting activities.

- *Eccentric action* is the opposite of concentric and is associated with the lengthening of the muscle as it contracts. Eccentric contractions are less common and are generally involved in the control of a movement-initiated concentric contraction. For example, during a soccer match when striking a ball, the quadriceps muscles contract concentrically to straighten the knee, but to coincide with this, the hamstrings contract eccentrically, decelerating the motion of the lower limb. However, this type of contraction places considerable strain through the muscle and is commonly related to muscle injuries.

Isometric: This type of muscle contraction

is associated with static exercise, where the muscle is still contracting, but no movement is produced: there is no lengthening or shortening of the muscle and no movement at the joints. For example, a soccer player may need to use isometric muscle action when holding off an opponent or shielding the ball. One benefit of isometric muscle actions is that they can be utilized for rehabilitation as well as general strength without placing any stress on the joints.

Isokinetic: This type of muscle action refers to muscular contraction at a constant speed over the full range of movement. Specialist equipment is needed to measure this type of movement, such as an isokinetic dynamometer. This type of muscular contraction is quite rare, and although this type of movement does not occur in general human activity, it is an effective way of improving muscular strength using specialized weight-training apparatus that provides a resistance equal to the force being applied by the performer. Isokinetic action can also be used in rehabilitation exercises to regain strength following injury.

The Energy Systems

Once the structure of the body is understood, and how the bones, joints and muscles work in unison to create movement, it is important to know what fuels the movement, enabling the contraction of muscles. Oxygen is obviously essential to the human body and to the contraction of muscles, but oxygen itself does not supply energy – its role is to allow the energy to be released from fuel stored in the muscle. In relation to soccer, which is a high intensity intermittent sport, the release of energy by oxygen is not fast enough to sustain performance. This is why the body

has different energy systems, depending upon the intensity of the exercise. There are three energy systems designed for immediate, short-term and long-term exercise.

Adenosine Triphosphate

Before we discuss the three energy systems, it is important to appreciate the role of adenosine triphosphate (ATP). ATP is a compound and is the only immediately usable form of energy stored in the body. We do, however, have other energy-rich compounds such as phosphocreatine and glycogen, but ATP is the only compound that can be utilized by the muscles to produce movement. ATP is stored in the muscle cell, which is the reason why it is so readily available; however, this is also problematic as it means only a very small amount of ATP can be stored in the body. ATP therefore needs to be resynthesized to continue exercising, and the body will use one of its three energy systems to do this, depending on the intensity of the exercise.

It is important to note that although these three energy systems will be discussed separately, they do not work in isolation. The amount of ATP resynthesized by each energy system will be limited by the intensity of exercise, and also two energy systems may be working at the same time to resynthesize ATP.

We will now look at each of the three systems in more detail, indicating both the advantages and disadvantages of each.

Immediate Energy: The Phosphocreatine System

This system is predominantly used for high intensity, short duration exercise requiring an immediate energy supply, for example a short sprint or an explosive jump for a header. This system uses a high energy compound called phosphocreatine (creatine (C) phosphate (P)), which provides the energy necessary to combine adenosine diphosphate (ADP) and phosphate (P). These chemical reactions take place in the muscle cell and do not need oxygen to proceed.

PC = P + C + Energy
Energy + ADP + P = ATP

The phosphocreatine system is very beneficial for an immediate release of energy, however there are some disadvantages as well: refer to the table for a breakdown of the main advantages and disadvantages of the phosphocreatine system.

Short-Term Energy: The Lactic Acid System

This is another anaerobic system that does not require oxygen to resynthesize ATP. The fuel necessary in this system is glycogen, which is found in foods, mainly carbohydrates. Carbohydrate is stored in the muscles and liver as glycogen, which is converted to glucose and undergoes a series of reactions known as 'anaerobic glycolysis'. This process resynthesizes two moles of ATP. However, due to the lack of oxygen, lactic acid is produced as a by-product, which can ultimately cause the muscles to fatigue. Refer to the table for a breakdown of the main advantages and disadvantages of the lactic acid system.

Long-Term Energy: The Aerobic System

In contrast to the previous two energy systems, the aerobic system requires oxygen as a fuel along with glycogen or fat in order to resynthesize ATP. This system is used when

Advantages and Disadvantages of the Phosphocreatine System

Advantages	Disadvantages
ATP resynthesis is provided very quickly	Only limited amounts of phosphocreatine can be stored in the muscle
As oxygen is not required, this eliminates any delay whilst oxygen is being supplied from the lungs	Only one mole of ATP can be resynthesized from one mole of phosphocreatine
Provides energy for very high intensity exercise	Only provides energy for a maximum of 10 seconds
Phosphocreatine will resynthesize relatively quickly, therefore recovery times between bouts of exercise are quite quick	
There are no harmful by-products to cause fatigue	

Advantages and Disadvantages of the Lactic Acid System

Advantages	Disadvantages
Relatively large amounts of glycogen are stored within the liver and muscles so this system can provide more ATP than the phosphocreatine system	Lactic acid is produced as a by-product, which increases the pH of the muscle cell, therefore making it more acidic. This can prevent chemical reactions and cause fatigue
ATP is provided quickly for high intensity activities lasting approximately 15 to 180 seconds	
As oxygen is not required, this eliminates any delay whilst oxygen is being supplied from the lungs	

Advantages and Disadvantages of the Aerobic System

Advantages	Disadvantages
36–38 moles of ATP can be resynthesized from one mole of glycogen	As oxygen is required, ATP resynthesis is not immediate: there is a delay whilst sufficient oxygen is transported to the working muscles
The aerobic system can sustain energy for activity for hours at a time	ATP cannot be resynthesized at high intensities
There are no harmful by-products from the chemical reactions	

exercise needs to be sustained for a longer period of time. Although it is not necessary to understand the complexities of the aerobic system, it is important to note that from one mole of glycogen, thirty-six to thirty-eight moles of ATP are produced.

Aerobic energy production is not just essential for long, endurance-based activities, it can also be beneficial in soccer where there is also a considerable demand placed on the aerobic system. Aerobic training can benefit high intensity, intermittent sports such as soccer because a well developed aerobic system helps to delay the onset of lactic acid accumulation in the muscle. Refer to the table for a breakdown of the main advantages and disadvantages of the aerobic system.

The Contribution of Each Energy System

As previously mentioned, although it may not be necessary for a soccer player or coach to possess a comprehensive knowledge of sport and exercise physiology, it is still important to understand the basic principles. Understanding which energy system will be in predominant use during exercise of different intensities will enable the coach to devise more effective

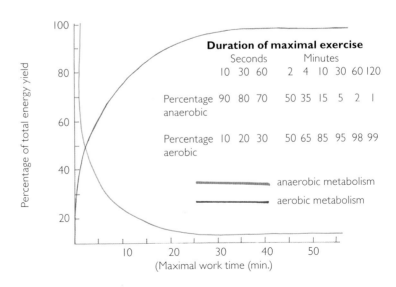

Fig. 10 Percentage contribution to total energy in relation to the duration of maximal work.

training programmes. For example, knowing that maximal effort can only be sustained for a relatively short duration, he or she will incorporate the necessary rest periods in the course of a high intensity plyometric session.

Although the three energy systems are described in isolation, in reality there is always a percentage contribution from both aerobic and anaerobic systems, which is why we will speak of 'the predominant energy system in use'. If we consider a soccer match, there is often a general amount of low intensity activity such as jogging back into position when the ball is out of play or when waiting for a free kick or throw-in to take place. In contrast, there are also times of explosive fast sprints when attacking or jumping for a header. During each of these activities energy is being supplied by all three energy systems, however the contribution of each system is determined by the intensity and duration of the exercise. Figure 10 demonstrates the percentage contribution to the total energy needed in relation to the duration of maximal work.

In general, if an activity is of very short duration – for example, sprinting for a few seconds – then the predominant energy system used for ATP resynthesis will be the phosphocreatine system. For an activity lasting up to one minute – for example a 400m run – the predominant energy system would be the lactic acid system. However, a significant contribution to ATP resynthesis would also come from the aerobic system, as there will be some oxygen available. Furthermore, there may also be a contribution from the phosphocreatine system if there is maximal effort at some point – for example, a sprint finish during the 400m run. Any activity lasting more than three minutes is generally considered to be predominantly using the aerobic system, depending on the individual's fitness levels.

CHAPTER 2

THE DEMANDS OF SOCCER

To plan an effective training programme it is essential to understand fully the nature of the sport and the physiological demands that coincide with it. The physiological demands of soccer are indicated by the exercise intensity with which the various activities are performed in match play. Gaining an appreciation of the intensity of exercise, and therefore which energy systems are prevalent in soccer, will ensure that training is directly relevant to the physiological demands in a match. As outlined in Chapter 1, understanding which energy system will be predominantly in use during different intensities will enable the coach to devise more effective training programmes. Therefore, utilizing direct information concerning the specific energy demands in a soccer match will highlight exactly which periods of the match are spent in low, moderate or high intensities, allowing the coach to replicate these conditions in training.

Furthermore, there is also a need to recognize the positional differences in soccer, and the variation in the characteristics needed to perform effectively, as certain positions may require specific training to improve a particular component of fitness.

This chapter will endeavour to highlight the various match intensities in soccer, as well as the impact of positional differences on energy demand. It will also discuss the onset of fatigue in matchplay, as well as focusing on the practical implications for coaches and players.

Match Intensities

Soccer is identified as high intensity, intermittent exercise, which heavily taxes the aerobic system. It requires players to move in multi directions at various speeds, which is why this activity is known as 'intermittent'. However, while the majority of exercise in football is at sub-maximal intensities, the importance of all-out efforts involving anaerobic metabolism should not be discounted. Often the successful execution of these high intensity activities determines the result of a game.

It is estimated that approximately 80 to 90 per cent of activity in a soccer match is aerobically fuelled, as the majority of the activity is concerned with movement off the ball, for example tracking the run of the opposition, or movement to create space whilst attacking. Aerobic fitness has been referred to as the determining factor for success in soccer due to the fact that fitter players are able to sustain a higher quality performance throughout the entire match. In contrast, all of the high intensity interactions with the ball will be predominantly fuelled anaerobically regardless of their duration. This indicates that although aerobic fitness may be directly linked to success in soccer, anaerobic energy production can also contribute to the outcome of a game due to the fact that all movements with the ball are determined by anaerobic metabolism, such as shots on goal.

In support of these claims, time-motion analysis of soccer has also found that approximately 80 to 90 per cent of performance is spent in low to moderate intensity activity, whereas the remaining 10 to 20 per cent is high intensity activity, therefore aerobic metabolism must predominate. However, soccer players have also been found to perform 150 to 250 brief intense actions during a game, equal to one every 90 seconds, highlighting the significance of anaerobic metabolism. Although it is clear that aerobic metabolism is the predominant source of energy delivery during a soccer match, it is interesting to note that the most decisive actions, which could determine the outcome of the game, are reliant on anaerobic metabolism. For example, the energy to perform actions such as short sprints, jumps, tackles and striking the ball is provided by anaerobic metabolism. Gaining knowledge based on the percentage of aerobic and anaerobic activity in a match can help the coach identify the most important fitness components on which to concentrate in train-ing. As will be discussed in Chapter 3, it is very important to ensure that training is specific to the physiological demands of the sport in order to create the correct adaptations and ultimately increase performance.

Distance Covered During a Match

The total distance covered by a player during a soccer match can provide approximate information on the amount of energy expended and the overall severity of the exercise. On average it is estimated that outfield players will cover between 9 to 14km, and goalkeepers approximately 4 to 6km. There are noticeable differences in the distance covered by outfield players; midfielders cover the greatest distances, whereas centre-backs have been found to cover the least distance compared to all other outfield players. The data that is being presented is based on elite-level soccer players, due to the limited studies in lower level soccer. However, the relative

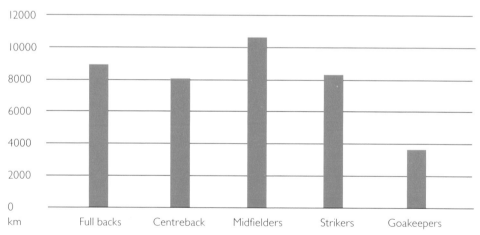

Fig. 11   The overall distance covered per game according to the player's positional role. (Source: Adapted from Reilly, T. and Thomas, V. (1976) 'A motion-analysis of work-rate in different positional roles in professional football match-play' Journal of Human Movement Studies, **2:** 87–97)

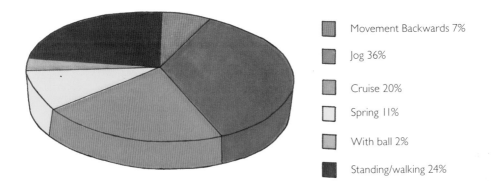

Movement Backwards 7%

Jog 36%

Cruise 20%

Spring 11%

With ball 2%

Standing/walking 24%

*Fig. 12   The relative distance covered by players in outfield positions according to categories of activity. (Source: Adapted from Reilly, T. and Thomas, V. (1976) 'A motion-analysis of work-rate in different positional roles in professional football match-play' Journal of Human Movement Studies, **2**: 87–97)*

positional differences will still be prevalent through all levels of soccer. Figure 11 highlights the positional differences in relation to the distances covered at elite level.

It is essential to acknowledge that the physiological demands imposed on soccer players are hugely variable; elements such as positional and tactical factors play a part, alongside game importance and quality of opponent. Furthermore, concentrating solely on the distance covered in a match may not provide the full picture of the specific demands of soccer, as it is the intensity of the effort expended when covering these distances which provides the information that coaches and players need in order to plan their training accordingly.

Breakdown of Distance Covered

It is of benefit to quantify the distances covered by each soccer position to help estimate the physical requirements and characteristics necessary for that position. However, possessing this information alone is quite a crude measure on which to base training:

what is essential for the coach to understand is what the distance covered actually equates to with regard to intensity, and how this can help inform their practice when designing training. Figure 12 demonstrates the total distance covered broken down into movement activities. Once again the information presented is based on elite-level data; however, the relative percentages will be similar throughout all levels. The activities are divided into standing/walking, jogging, cruising (running with manifest purpose and effort), sprinting, moving backwards, and time with the ball.

It is interesting to observe that in a 90-minute game of soccer, a player only has possession of the ball for 2 per cent of the total time, which equates to approximately 108 seconds. Although the time on the ball may seem extremely low, when put into context the typical interaction with the ball is a one-touch pass or quick control followed by a pass. Players will generally receive the ball with approximately one to five metres of space between them and the opposition, with half a second or less to execute a skill. Therefore it is imperative to note that although time on the ball may be relatively limited, this does not mean that it is less important to work on ball work and skill development in training – in fact it emphasizes the complete opposite, and it is essential to dedicate time to perfect ballwork skills due to the limited amount of time each player has the ball in their possession.

This is particularly significant at the higher level as they may only get one or two opportunities to complete a decisive through-ball, or to strike the ball at goal to hopefully influence the end result, so their technique must be of a high enough standard to take advantage of these opportunities when they arise. Nevertheless, unsurprisingly the overall activity profile of soccer indicates that most exercise is conducted off the ball at sub-maximal intensity. These low and moderate intensity activities will generally consist of tactics such as supporting runs, tracking back into position when play breaks down, and so on. However, it is the high intensity elements in the match, albeit less frequent, that are associated with crucial events that can directly affect the outcome.

On average players carry out high-intensity effort, either cruise or sprint, every 30 seconds, and sprint maximally every 90 seconds. Generally sprints have been found to last on average 4 seconds, equating to a mean distance of approximately 25 to 30 metres, with average rest periods of approximately 40 to 60 seconds. These are interesting figures which can help determine how a coach will design soccer drills to ensure they are specific to the demands of the sport, with regard to distances and rest intervals. Gaining this knowledge will help the coach eliminate drills that are unnecessary for soccer and therefore excessive.

Obviously these results are based on average findings, and there will be circumstances where sprints will be required for longer or shorter periods, as soccer is an unpredictable sport. For example, although the average rest period is approximately 40 to 60 seconds, sometimes a rest period may last for as long as three minutes, while on other occasions a player may experience almost no rest for a few minutes, depending on the nature of that particular period in the game. The difficult challenge for players and coaches is to be able to train specifically for these high intensity, short duration bouts – bearing in mind that acceleration and deceleration can add significantly to the overall energy cost – and to recover effectively in a relatively short period to repeat the exercise again.

Positional Differences

The Defender
Defenders have been found to perform the highest amount of backward movement, especially high intensity backward and lateral movement, which requires an elevated energy expenditure of approximately 20 to 40 per cent in comparison to forward running. Defenders are also involved in significantly more situations where they are required to jump and head the ball, as they are diving in feet first when attempting to intercept passes or block shots and crosses. However, although defenders may have to expend more energy due to their higher amount of backward and lateral movement, they have also been found to engage in significantly lower levels of sprinting and cruising as compared to other positions. Furthermore, defenders perform the highest amount of low level activity such as jogging, skipping and shuffling.

Midfielders
Midfielders have been found to partake in activity of low to moderate intensity more frequently and for longer durations, and are

stationary for considerably less time than any other outfield player. The result of these types of movement pattern equates to midfielders covering the greatest overall distances during match play. Midfielders also spend the most time cruising or sprinting, and experience higher levels of time on the ball.

Strikers

Strikers are required to be physically the strongest player, as it has been found that they are involved in the most physical contact at high intensity. They are subject to a high degree of pushing and pulling activities in the upper body, therefore strength is an advantage, so they can withstand this type of pressure. Strikers have also been found to engage in higher levels of sudden stopping at high intensities, as well as changing direction and decelerating more rapidly. Similar to midfielders, strikers also experience high levels of possession actions and almost the same levels of sprinting; they also perform a significantly higher amount of shuffling movements. This may be explained by the difference in spatial and time demands within these two positions.

Although all outfield players are engaged in essentially the same soccer match, there are obvious differences in the requirements of the different positions in match play. Understanding the physical requirements of the positions will enable the coach to identify which players may be more suited to certain positions, and also – more importantly – to identify the areas of improvement or development that are required in order to perform effectively in that particular position.

Fatigue in Soccer

Fatigue can be defined as a decline in performance as a result of having to continue the activity being performed. Fatigue in soccer is generally associated by a decline in work rate towards the end of the game. There is evidence to suggest that the overall distance covered is approximately 5 per cent less in the second half of the match as compared to the first. When analysing the physical demands of soccer is it important to focus on the detrimental effects of fatigue and the direct impact on performance. If a player is not at the correct fitness level he will not be able to sustain the demands of a match. Even a drop in performance of approximately 5 per cent may mean losing half a second of speed, or a decrease in power for explosive actions such as shots, tackles or blocks. Winning and losing in soccer is separated by these small margins, which is why a considerable amount of time is allocated to training the player in the physical aspects of the game. This is also why research is conducted into the specific physical demands of soccer, so that coaches can identify the physiological level their players need to attain in order to avoid the onset of fatigue.

It is no coincidence that teams with the highest fitness levels are often the teams that score during the final fifteen minutes of a soccer match, when the team with a lower level of fitness may be experiencing the onset of fatigue. Figure 13 shows all the goals scored in the Premier League in the 2010/2011 season, and it is clear to see that the highest percentage of goals scored are within the last fifteen minutes of the game: this serves to highlight the importance of being able to sustain performance for the full ninety minutes. The ability to apply pressure on the opponent and reduce the time they have to make critical decisions and decisive actions will be lost during the latter stages of the match if fitness levels are not sufficient. The outcome of the game may be won or lost during this critical period in a match, therefore coaches need to be aware of the physiological conditioning of their team.

Scoring Times (Overall)

Minutes	Goals	% goals
0–15	138	13.0%
16–30	156	14.7%
31–45	182	17.1%
46–60	175	16 5%
61–75	165	15.5%
76–90	247	23.2%

Fig. 13   The timing of goals scored in the 2010/2011 Premier League season.

Fatigue is not only present during the latter stages of a match, but players may also experience periods of fatigue momentarily during a game. Studies have demonstrated that in a game, after constant high intensity periods of up to five minutes without any recovery time, players' performance can be reduced by 12 per cent for the ensuing five minutes. This type of fatigue is only temporary, however, and the rate of recovery will depend on the individual's level of aerobic fitness.

'Mental fatigue' is also apparent in match play in the form of lapses in concentration due to the level of physical effort needed to sustain performance. These lapses in concentration may become apparent in areas such as decision-making, where errors may provide the opponents with a goal-scoring opportunity, or may even prevent the player from capitalizing on a goal-scoring opportunity. Towards the latter stages of the game, play generally becomes more urgent if a team is pressing for an equalizer or a winning

goal despite the physical capabilities of the player, which explains why maintaining concentration can become increasingly important.

Specific studies have attempted to identify the effects of fatigue on sprint performance in soccer matches. Figure 14 shows the decline in sprint performance towards the end of a match. Players' repeat sprint performances were measured over a distance of 30m either during the first half of a match, the second half, or at the end of it. Players were required to complete five consecutive 30sec sprints with a 30sec recovery between each bout. It is clear to see in Figure 14 that sprint performance is visibly reduced in the second half, and further reduced post match.

If we look at this from a practical perspective and apply it to a match situation, this means that a 30m sprint performed in the first half may take approximately 3.8sec, however towards the end of the second half the same 30m sprint may now take 4.1sec. Although this might not seem significant, in fact it equates to a difference of 8 per cent, which equates to approximately 2m that a player would concede due to the onset of fatigue. For example, a midfielder might execute a through-ball to the striker in behind the defender in the 87th minute of a match. If the defender is experiencing the onset of fatigue but the striker is not, then the striker may have a 2m advantage with regard to sprint performance, enabling him to avoid any attempt at a tackle by the defender, as well as escaping pressure on the ball, allowing the striker a clear strike on goal, which could equate to a match-winning opportunity.

You may be familiar with the phrase 'the game has opened up': this may be due to one team figuring out the opponent's tactics, or having to take greater risks due to conceding a goal. However, one major factor in a 'game opening up' can be attributed to the onset of fatigue. There may not be as much pressure on the ball as the player was previously experiencing, or suddenly a run into space is no longer tracked by the opponent. Teams with the higher level of fitness will utilize this period in a game. Furthermore, the introduction of substitutions during these stages can be optimal to exploit the new space created, since players with 'fresh legs' will have a distinct advantage over opponents who are experiencing fatigue, allowing them to ultimately affect the outcome of the game. As previously mentioned, winning and losing in soccer is defined by small margins, and identifying training programmes to avoid the onset of fatigue will give players an advantage, especially in the latter stages of a match.

Practical Applications for Training

Throughout this chapter it is clear to see that soccer is a high intensity intermittent activity comprising a variety of multi-directional movements, encompassing low, moderate and high intensity periods. The demands of match play place a number of physiological stresses on the body, most of which are general to all players; however, as already mentioned, there are certain attributes specific to certain positions. To cope with these demands successfully, players must undertake training based specifically around the movement patterns that have been identified as necessary to ensure that the training is fully transferable to the match-play environment. The programme must incorporate both aerobic and anaerobic fitness training in order to deal with all aspects

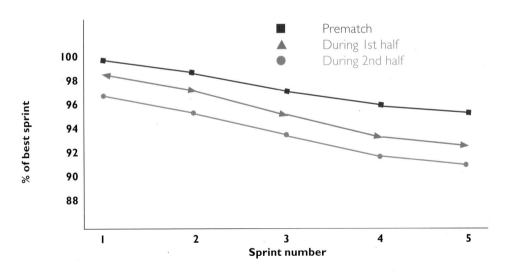

Fig. 14   Repeated sprint test before and during the first half, and during the second half of a soccer match. (Courtesy Krustrup, P., Mohr, M., Steensberg, A., Bencke, J., Kjear, M., and Bangsbo, J. (2006) 'Muscle and Blood Metabolites during a Soccer Game: Implications for Sprint Performance' Medicine and Science in Sport and Exercise, **38:** 1165–1174)

of soccer. It has been identified that on average players carry out high-intensity effort, either cruise or sprint, every thirty seconds, and sprint maximally every ninety seconds.

This type of information is key for coaches when including anaerobic sprint exercises, as well as knowing to allow for adequate rest periods. Generally sprints have been found to last on average four seconds, equating to a mean distance of approximately 25 to 30m, with average rest periods of approximately 40 to 60sec. These figures can help determine how a coach will design soccer drills to ensure they are specific to the demands of the sport, with regard to distances and rest intervals.

Coaches need to be able to interpret the information gained in terms of the positional characteristics and the prevailing differences. For example, it has been found that both strikers and defenders need to be physically strong, as they are involved in the most physical contact at high intensity, such as heading, tackling and holding off opponents. This

therefore indicates that muscular power will need to be developed in training, so players can execute explosive actions such as jumping and acceleration. Specific exercises on aerobic and anaerobic fitness training will be outlined in more detail in chapters 4 to 6.

It is also important to emphasize that although ensuring players have optimal fitness levels to be able to cope with the demands of soccer and to avoid the onset of fatigue, dedicating time in training to develop technique and skill on the ball should not be underestimated. As we have seen, out of a 90-minute game of soccer, a player only has possession of the ball for 2 per cent of the total time, which equates to approximately 108 seconds. Out of context this figure seems extremely low; however, it is within this 2 per cent that goals are scored and created. Overall, dedicating sufficient time to skill development, as well as incorporating all-round fitness for soccer, requires that a variety of elements is included in the training programme of all players.

CHAPTER 3

THE PRINCIPLES OF TRAINING FOR SOCCER

The overall aim of athletes is to achieve their athletic goal, whether that be an Olympic gold medal or to win the Premier League. But whatever the aim, in order to achieve it the athlete must undertake a structured training programme. In sport there is no such thing as a 'one size fits all' training programme that will significantly improve performance. In soccer training alone there are many different types and variations of training methods used, although not every training method will be practical for each individual. While there is no such thing as a standard programme for everyone, there are, however, certain rules that underpin all training methods, known as the 'principles of training'. We will discuss specific types of training in the upcoming chapters, but before we look at precise training design, it is important to understand the principles of training and how these link together ultimately to improve performance.

The Principles of Training

Specificity

It is not uncommon for athletes who consider themselves fit for a certain sport to find it difficult to sustain performance in others. For example, a 100m sprinter who may be able to complete the 100m in under ten seconds would still struggle to complete a marathon without specific training in that area. This illustrates that training for one sport, whatever the level athletes are competing at, does not necessarily mean they are fit for another sport with different physiological demands.

Specificity is the principle of training that proposes that sports training should be relevant and appropriate to the sport for which the individual is training in order to produce a training effect. The specificity principle simply states that training must progress from highly general to highly specific, thus implying that in order to become better at a particular exercise or skill it is essential to perform it. For example, although soccer is a high intensity, intermittent sport – as outlined in Chapter 2 – a general level of stamina is still required, but in order to train stamina for soccer it would be inappropriate to conduct all stamina training on bikes, as this would not be specific to the type of stamina exercise that would be required in a game of soccer. This is why a knowledge of the demands of the sport is important, to fully understand why and how to plan and deliver training.

It is imperative to develop training programmes specific to soccer in order to gain functional improvements, although it would be naïve to believe that all other forms of training would be detrimental to soccer. There is a concept known as 'transfer of training', which refers to a gain in one component of fitness as a direct result of training for another. For example, a soccer player is perhaps only training their aerobic capacity, concentrating solely on their stamina, but if their training programme is analysed by a coach they might indicate that speed, muscular strength and power are also important. So although the soccer player has not been directly training for the anaerobic components, it is conceivable that there will still have been some physiological adaptation in these components as a result of the current aerobic training they are doing, albeit not as prevalent as if they had been training the anaerobic component directly.

The 'transfer of training' effect may be present in some generalized programmes, which will obviously be beneficial; however, it is important to note that ultimately when designing a training programme it must be specific to the sport and the individual in order to get the best results. Factors such as age, ability, current level of fitness and positions should also be considered when planning the specificity of training.

Progression

In the initial stage of training players are sometimes over-enthusiastic and want to push themselves in order to progress and develop their skills and fitness. This enthusiasm is obviously beneficial for motivation, but it can also be detrimental if it leads to excessive training, resulting in fatigue and burnout. High intensity work too soon can cause injury and have damaging effects on the body. The principle of progression is an important component of training programmes, and suggests that there is an optimal level of overload that should be achieved, and an optimal time frame for this overload to occur.

Overload refers to the amount of work in a training session, and is discussed in more detail next. Overload should not be increased too slowly, or improvement is unlikely. Furthermore, when the level of training is increased too rapidly it can be counterproductive and

may result in injury or muscle damage. For example, a player may be returning to training after a long-term injury and is frustrated that they are not attaining the levels of fitness they once had. Increasing the intensity and frequency of their training load would not be productive and may actually have negative effects on their fitness levels, whilst risking a recurrence of the injury. The principle of progression emphasizes the need for proper rest and recovery, as ultimately that is when the adaptations occur, not during the training session. Continual stress on the body and constant overload will result in exhaustion and injury. It is imperative not to train hard all the time, as doing so will lead to overtraining, and a great deal of physical and psychological damage will result.

As previously mentioned, there is no 'one size fits all' training programme and this also applies with regard to the rate of progression. It is not possible to be specific about the rate of progression and the length of time you should wait before incorporating the progression, as each individual responds differently. However, it is down to the player or coach to monitor training loads, and decide how and when progression is necessary for the individual.

Overload

The purpose of training is to improve in the specified area relevant to performance. In life the human body is involved in a constant process of adapting to stresses or lack of stresses placed upon it, and adapting accordingly. When designing a training programme it will be necessary to incorporate exercises/drills that will stress the body in a manner it is unaccustomed to (overload), thus ensuring that it will react, thereby causing physiological changes (adaptation): it will then be better able to handle that stress the next time it occurs.

The human body likes to be in a state of homeostasis, which basically means 'remaining stable' or 'in a balanced state'. The principle of overload attempts to disrupt the body's homeostasis, and implies that in order for the required training adaptation to take place, a greater than normal stress or load on the body is needed – that is, greater than would be expected in day-to-day life or in a general training session. This is necessary because the body will only adapt to a new stimulus, which is greater than the one it is currently experiencing.

Once the body has adapted then an even greater stimulus is required in order to continue the change. For example, in order for a muscle to increase in strength, it must be gradually stressed by working against a load greater than it is used to. Furthermore, to increase endurance, muscles must work for a longer period of time than they are used to. Therefore if you are repeating a training session of the same intensity over and over again, the body will have made the required adaptations already, and all you will be doing is simply maintaining the current fitness level, not increasing fitness levels. In addition, if this stress is removed or decreased there may also be a decrease in that particular component of fitness. Therefore it is important to incorporate the principle of progression, as this will help indicate how and when to increase the training load.

It is essential to remember that individuals will respond to training stimuli differently, and that they do not all adapt at the same rate. There are many factors that dictate the rate of adaptation, such as genetics, physiological make-up and current fitness levels, which will all impact on the tolerance of training programmes. This reinforces the need for specificity, not only to the particular sport but also for the individual. A relatively sedentary or unfit person will initially adapt rapidly as even the smallest overload in stimulus will be an increase on current activity. However, as the individual becomes progressively fitter, the adaptation process will be considerably slower. It is beneficial for players and coaches to understand this concept, as this will help regulate the motivation of the athlete and prevent disappointment when adaptation seems to be minimal.

An effective training programme will endeavour to introduce a new effective overload when required, so as to produce adaptations that ensure the athletes are progressing. There are different ways of manipulating the training overload, such as frequency and intensity.

Frequency

'Frequency' relates to the number of training sessions that occur within a specified timeframe. The frequency of training depends on a number of factors, such as current fitness levels, the stage of athlete development, and the training phase. Frequency also refers to incorporating the optimal amounts of exercise, because it is a fine balance between providing just enough stress for the body to adapt to, and allowing enough time for healing and adaptation to occur. How often you exercise is an important aspect of fitness in order to make safe yet continuing progress. For example, frequency may be used as an overload during pre-season when there is more time to recover since there are no competitive matches – so additional training sessions would help increase the stress placed on the body in order to produce adaptations.

Intensity

Intensity of training refers to the concept of how hard an athlete should train, or the amount of effort that should be invested in a training programme, or in any one session. Similar to frequency there is an obvious need to find the optimal balance between finding enough intensity to overload the body to produce adaptations, but not too much, therefore avoiding the negative aspects of overtraining. The intensity of a session is required to be both sport and training session specific. Depending upon the aims of that particular session you can structure the intensity of a session to concentrate on either aerobic or anaerobic fitness components – as discussed in Chapter 2, the intensity of exercise dictates which energy system you predominantly use. Knowledge of the intensity necessary to achieve adaptations in either aerobic or anaerobic exercise is an important aspect to consider when planning a session, so as to initiate the required response.

Reversibility

The principle of reversibility is essentially the opposite of adaptation. Not only do athletes not maintain their fitness levels when they stop training, they can also decrease their fitness levels. Reversibility dictates that athletes lose the effects of training when they stop training as fitness levels can drop quickly when periods of inactivity occur. However, this does not mean that the fitness levels are lost forever, as the detraining effects can be reversed when they resume training once again.

It is essential to appreciate that it is certainly not advisable to remove any periods of rest from the training plan, as rest periods are essential to allow the training-induced adaptations to occur. However, times of extended rest intervals will result in reduced physical fitness, because the physiological effects of fitness training diminish over time, causing the body to revert to its pre-training condition. It is therefore important that training programmes do not incorporate any long periods of inactivity; even during the off-season it would be advisable to take part in

some form of physical activity, albeit in a more recreational context.

Variance

As discussed in the principles of training previously outlined, a combination of a specified training programme incorporating a planned progression and periods of overload is essential in order to gain the optimal adaptations ultimately to increase performance. Furthermore, due to the negative effects associated with prolonged levels of inactivity, training must be a continuous progressive cycle – though obviously incorporating adequate rest periods when required. However, training can lack excitement and be portrayed as tedious, so it is essential to vary your approach to training.

The principle of variance refers to the need to implement minor changes in training programmes to produce more consistent gains in sport performance. Training programmes for soccer should include variations in the manipulations of intensity, frequency, progression, and other important aspects of practice. Introducing a variety of training sessions, which are carefully planned to avoid repetition, is vital in order to maintain motivation and commitment. Furthermore, varying sessions will also help to avoid injuries incurred by over-use.

One of the most recognized strategies that adheres to the principle of variability is periodization, which is concerned with training in phases. Periodization is an organized approach to training which involves the progressive cycling of various aspects of a training programme during a specific period of time. It is a way of alternating training to its peak during the season by designing training programmes in areas such as preparatory, competitive and transition phases. Specific details of how to create a periodized training programme will be outlined in Chapter 8.

CHAPTER 4

AEROBIC TRAINING FOR SOCCER

Aerobic training is an integral part of an effective soccer-training regime. It provides the players with a base level of fitness, which is essential because they are required to run for long periods of time. The game itself demands that players are active for forty-five minutes per half, and up to 120 minutes in total during periods of extra time; thus they need a good endurance capacity in order to deal with the extended periods of running required in the course of the game. The increased aerobic capacity will enable each player to make a quick recovery from sprints associated with the game of soccer, and will strengthen muscles and tendons as a bi-product of the training. Whilst it is important that we train for soccer and not the marathon – that is, we take into account the exact nature of the events associated with match play – it is imperative that the aerobic system is considered and trained appropriately to ensure a well rounded approach to soccer-specific fitness. Research has demonstrated that it is beneficial for players to have a greater aerobic fitness, as this will result in an increase in distances covered with more sprints during a game.

This chapter will explain the training aspect associated with the aerobic energy pathway. The varying forms of aerobic training will be outlined, followed by practical training exercises that can be employed to develop this aspect. However, before the aerobic training methodologies can be discussed and applied, it is important to ensure that the body prepares itself to deal with the training stimulus; therefore attention will first be given to effective warm-up and cool-down techniques.

Preparing for Physical Activity: The Warm-Up

Before engaging players in any form of training it is vital that the body is prepared for the rigours that are to follow. A coach should always ensure that the players follow a warm-up that advances in intensity and focuses on key muscles that are associated with soccer training. The warm-up should consist of two phases: a pulse raiser, and stretching the muscles.

The pulse raiser should do exactly that – raise the pulse. It is called such because the pulse is an indicator of heart rate, and when the pulse is raised the heart is beating faster, which increases the flow of blood (and therefore oxygen) around the body. Conducting a pulse raiser will raise the core body temperature and increase the blood flow around the muscles. The increase in body temperature will help to increase the flexibility of the muscles, and therefore helps to prevent soft tissue injuries as a result of the increased range of motion now available round the joints. The activity should develop in intensity as the session approaches, with soccer-specific stretching following the pulse raiser.

Stretches used at this stage are done to help prepare the player for the game, and should reflect the activities in the game, such as running, jumping, turning and lunging. In order to achieve this, dynamic stretching is utilized. Dynamic stretching is essentially stretching on the move: it replicates the active movements associated with the game of soccer and will lead to an increase in range of movement around a joint. In the game of soccer it is important that the whole body is prepared, and as such the stretching phase should integrate both the upper and lower body. A sample dynamic stretching protocol is included below.

- Players increasing their core body temperature
- An increase in heart rate and therefore blood flow
- An increase in breathing rate
- Improved suppleness of the muscular system
- Preparation of the body for activity
- Psychological preparation for the game

Pulse-raising Activities

Where possible a warm-up should be conducted with the football in order to engross the players in the activity: this will help to engage them, and will provide a stimulating environment for them, which in turn will help to prepare their psychological state and mental alertness. It is recommended that

the pulse-raising element of the warm-up is at least five minutes in length. Below are some suggested activities for raising the heart rate – but remember that the intensity should be raised progressively.

Ball Steal

Mark out a 20 × 20 grid with four cones, as seen in Fig. 15 (retain this grid as it will be used for the dynamic stretching that follows the pulse-raising activity). Split the players evenly, if possible, into four groups and direct

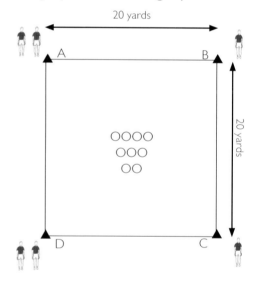

Fig. 15   Ball steal.

each group to a different cone (cones A to D). Place nine footballs in the middle of the grid. Players attempt to get three balls back to their cone in order to be crowned the winners. However, only one player at a time goes and retrieves a ball, and he must 'high five' the next player before they can leave. Balls should be dribbled back once retrieved, and players are allowed to steal balls from other cones.

The Quadathlon

This exercise is called the quadathlon as the players must perform four tasks. The players are split into groups: there can be anything from one to four groups, depending how many are taking part in the session. In the 20 × 20 grid, create four quadrants, using different colour cones to identify them (see Fig. 16).

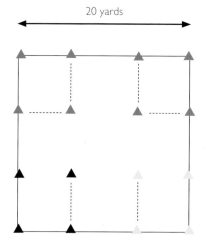

20 yards

Fig. 16 The quadathlon.

Each player is given a football, and each group is designated a quadrant to start in.

The coach will dictate a set task to be completed in each quadrant: this is fairly flexible, and he or she can choose almost anything for the players to do. For example, in the blue quadrant players might complete ten keepy-upees without the ball touching the floor. In the green quadrant they might complete ten passes with each player in their group. In the red quadrant they might dribble the ball around each cone outlining the quadrant, and back to the middle five times; and

in the yellow quadrant they might dribble to the edge of the quadrant and then perform five turns with the inside of their foot, before dribbling to the other side of the quadrant and performing five turns with the outside of the foot.

Once the players have completed the task in each of the quadrants the group dribbles to the next quadrant, moving in a clockwise direction.

This activity is extremely flexible and can be repeated multiple times, or the tasks changed on each lap, or it might use a competition format where the first team back to the quadrant they started in, having completed all the tasks, is declared the winner.

Numbers

Numbers is an extremely simplistic game that is easy to set up, explain and manage. Each player has a football and stands in the 20 ×

20 yards

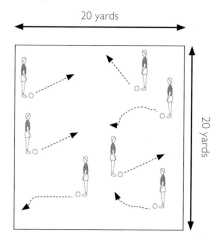

20 yards

Fig. 17 Numbers.

20 grid in a space. The players then dribble the football around the grid whilst avoiding all the other players and their footballs. Players should be encouraged to keep changing direc-

tion throughout, and they can do this using any turn of their choosing or as directed by the coach. When the coach calls out a number the players must quickly form groups of this number (for instance if the coach shouts three, players must get into groups of three). All players start with five lives, and any player who does not manage to end up in a group of the size stipulated by the coach loses a life.

Dynamic Stretches

Mark out a 20 × 20 grid with cones. Players start each exercise from side A of the grid, and repeat each movement until they reach side B (see Fig. 18). Once at side B, they start the next exercise working towards side A of the grid. Players continue to work between each side of the grid until all the dynamic stretches have been completed. Coaches should be mindful to stress the importance of good form, as players do tend to rush through each exercise to get to the other side of the grid, and so sacrifice the quality of the movement. This impacts on the effectiveness of the movement, and so players should be encouraged to follow the points below for each exercise.

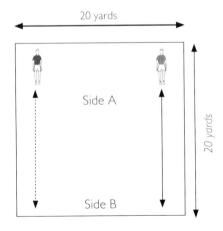

Fig. 18   Stretching grid.

Trunk Rotations

With the feet anchored to the floor and toes and hips pointing forwards, rotate around the spine without moving the hips. Let the head lead the movement and the trunk will follow. This should be completed to the left before

Trunk rotations.

coming back to the midline, and then to the right. Players should then take two steps towards side B of the grid, and repeat the exercise.

Knee Rolls

Lie on your back and pull your knees to your chest. Lock the hands together behind the knees and then roll forwards and backwards, keeping the back in contact with the floor. After completing, stand up and jog through to the other side of the grid in preparation for the next exercise.

Knee rolls.

High Kick

With the left arm reaching forwards and parallel to the floor, kick the right leg across the body to touch the left hand. Ensure the leg comes to the hand, and not the hand to the leg! Players should jog two steps before repeating for the left leg.

Hamstring Swings

For this exercise it will be necessary to hold on to a partner or a goal frame for support. Standing upright and with the goal frame in the left hand, kick the left leg forwards until it reaches parallel with the floor, and then swing behind you in a continuous motion. Continue this movement for ten repetitions on each leg.

Hamstring swings.

Open the Gate

Raise the knee until the thigh is parallel to the floor with the knee bent at 90 degrees. Then push the knee out to the side until it is aligned to the rest of the body. This should be a smooth action and should mimic the opening of a gate. Then return the leg to the floor. Alternate between legs whilst working from one side of the grid to the other.

High kick.

Open the gate..

High Skip
From a start position standing on the balls of the feet, drive one knee up whilst also driving

High skip.

the opposite arm to perform a skipping-type motion. Drive both hand and knee vertically to gain as much height as possible. Alternate the driving knee, and continue until arriving at the opposite side of the grid.

Heel Flicks
Whilst retaining a jogging position with the upper body, place the back of the hands on the buttocks. Whilst jogging from one side of the grid to the other, raise the heels to touch the hands in a continuous motion.

Heel flicks.

Walking Lunge
With the upper body in an upright position with a strong core, step forwards with the right leg and lower the hips to the floor. The leading leg should be at 90 degrees with the thigh parallel to the floor: hold for three seconds, then stand upright. Repeat for each leg whilst moving across the grid.

Walking lunge.

Sumos

Perform this stretch whilst side on to the direction you are travelling in. With the feet shoulder-width apart and pointing slightly out,

Sumos.

lower the hips to the floor whilst maintaining a neutral back position. Try to ensure that the thighs are parallel with the floor before returning to an upright position. Bring the trail leg through and repeat until the other side of the grid is reached.

Hamstring Walk

With the feet hip-width apart, place both hands on the shoulders. Place one leg in front of the other and raise the toes. Slowly lower the hips to the floor whilst bending the back leg, keeping the back straight and looking

Hamstring walk.

forwards. Keep moving forwards, and work both legs by alternating the lead leg.

Arm Rotations

Extend the arms out to the side, and then begin to draw circles with the fingers. Gradually increase the size of the circles. Conduct this exercise in both a forward and backward direction.

Arm rotations.

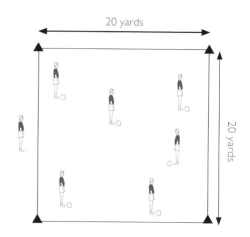

Fig. 19 Traffic lights.

Cooling Down

Once the training session or match is complete it is important to complete a cool-down to help the body return to its natural resting state. In the same way that the warm-up raised the body temperature and increased the heart rate to prepare for activity, it is important to ensure that this is reversed during the cool-down by steadily lowering the intensity of exercise. This steady reduction in intensity will not only lower the core body temperature but will also prevent blood 'pooling'. Blood-pooling occurs when activity is stopped abruptly and the heart rate is not decreased gradually. It is typified by dizziness and nausea, and if players report these symptoms then an inadequate cool-down may be the cause.

Pulse-Lowering Activities

Traffic Lights
In a 20 × 20 grid, as used in the pulse-raising activities, players are asked to dribble the football around and keep changing direction. They should be instructed that this should be done at no more than jogging speed. The coach should have three cones in the hand,

red, yellow and green in colour, to mimic a set of traffic lights. Each cone will mean something slightly different, and when the coach holds each one up, the players should respond accordingly. Whenever the coach lowers the cone, players will return to dribbling around the grid.

For example, when the red cone is elevated, players stop with their foot on the ball. When the yellow cone is raised, they turn with the ball (a turn of their choice or as stipulated by the coach) and walk with the ball at their feet until the cone is lowered, when they continue jogging. When the green cone is held up they accelerate forwards with the ball. The coach will move between each cone as he sees fit, but as this exercise is aimed at cooling the players down, it would be beneficial to have more green cone activities early on, with more yellow and red activities towards the end of the cool-down.

Volley and Catch
The players are split into two teams, and play a game where they attempt to get ten passes together in order to score a goal. However,

they can only pass the ball from their hands using a volley, and it must be caught by the person they have passed to. The team in possession is attacking, whilst the other team is defending, and the defending team will attempt to intercept the ball – and if they do they will become the attacking team. If the defending team 'tags' a player of the attacking team when they are in possession of the ball, then there is a turnover and the defending team becomes the attacking team. If the ball is dropped, or the pass is not completed, then again there is a turnover in possession.

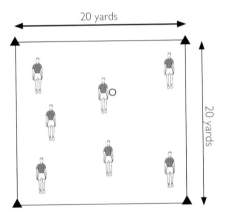

Fig. 20   Volley and catch.

As this exercise is competitive the players will be working hard and running around. However, as the focus of this activity is on cooling down, the coach should run the activity at normal pace for the first few minutes, and then state that players can only walk (that is, they must have one limb in contact with the floor at all times) and any running will result in a goal and turnover of possession. Finally, in an attempt to lower the intensity still further, the coach should stipulate that players cannot move with the ball in their hands.

Musical Soccer

Players are to dribble around the grid at a jogging pace. They should keep avoiding each other and looking for space by keeping their heads up and looking where they are going. When the coach shouts 'change' they must each stop their football, leave it where it is, and go and find another ball. Once they have another ball they continue to dribble.

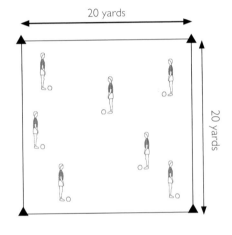

Fig. 21   Musical soccer.

Allow the players a few attempts at this, then remove one of the balls and instruct that player to jog around the grid without a ball. This time when the coach shouts 'change' there will be one person left without a ball and that person will lose a life. They will continue to jog around the grid and will attempt to find a ball the next time the coach calls 'change'. In order to lower the intensity of the exercise the coach can manage the workload of players by instructing them to jog and walk at different points, as in the previous two activities.

Static Stretches

An effective cool-down will include stretching the muscles to avoid soreness and tightness.

A sample battery of static stretching exercises is included below. These should be held for 15–20sec per exercise. Where this is for each limb, perform the exercise on both sides.

Hamstrings

With the feet hip-width apart, place both hands on the shoulders. Place one leg in front of the other, and raise the toes. Slowly lower the hips to the floor whilst bending the back leg and keeping the back straight. Remember to keep the head up and look forwards. Repeat the exercise with the opposite leg in front.

Starting from a kneeling position, push the buttocks back to the heels. Keep the hands in their original position and tuck the head underneath the body.

Back stretch 1.

Hamstrings stretch.

Back stretch 2.

Back

Lie on the stomach in a flat position. Place the hands adjacent to the shoulders (replicating the starting position of a press-up) and slowly lift the head whilst keeping the hips in contact with the ground.

Groins

Whilst seated on the floor, bend the legs and place the soles of the feet together. Grasp each ankle in the hands, and then with elbows on knees, push the elbows to the floor whilst keeping the soles of the feet together.

Fig. 22   Groin stretch.

Quadriceps

Grasp the right ankle in the right hand, and pull the heel towards the buttocks. Ensure that you are standing in an upright position, and push the right hip forwards. Repeat these steps for the left leg.

Quadriceps stretch.

Calves

You will need a goal frame or wall for this exercise. Starting about one metre away from the goal frame, take a step towards the goal with the right leg. Lean forwards, placing all your weight over the right leg, and lean into the goal frame. With a straight back leg you will begin to feel the stretch in the lower part of the leg. Be sure to keep the heel on the floor to get maximum benefit from the stretch.

Calf stretch.

Arms and Shoulders

Place the right hand across the chest, and with the left arm gently pull the right arm further across the body.

Stretch the right hand up towards the sky and then bend at the elbow, placing the palm directly between the shoulder blades. Bring the left hand over on to the elbow and use this to apply gentle pressure to enable the palm to reach further down the back.

Arm and shoulder stretch 1.

Arm and shoulder stretch 2.

Neck
Standing upright with the shoulders back, rest the chin on the chest.

From the same starting position, raise the chin to the sky.

Develop this by looking over each shoulder. Remember this is a stretching exercise, and as such it should be possible to feel the stretch

Neck stretch downwards.

Neck stretch upwards.

– so be sure you are working to maintain the stretch for the entire duration.

Neck stretch to the side.

Chest

Clasp the hands together behind the back, and roll the shoulders backwards. Gently push the hands away from the body, and hold the position when you feel the stretch.

Chest stretch.

Aerobic Training Methodologies

Aerobic fitness can be trained in a number of forms: these are discussed in this section, in addition to practical examples of each type of training that can be used in day-to-day training. One interesting point to note is that in many of these examples a football is used. Almost any skill-based drill can be developed so that the physiological system is also developed, and this is an integral part of getting the most from players. Research has identified that introducing a football to fitness training drills raises the training stimulus, as the players are more attracted to drills performed with the ball than drills without. This is particularly important when maximal effort is required over a period of time in a tough training session: using a football can ensure maximal adaptation.

Continuous Training

Continuous training works the aerobic system by using exercises that are more than twenty minutes (and up to two hours) in duration, and which are typified by the fact that the exercise is performed without rest intervals during this time. Accordingly the intensity of exercise is low to medium, and as a rule of thumb, the athlete should be able to talk whilst working through the exercise without undue respiratory distress.

The body uses its aerobic energy stores to improve overall fitness and endurance. In the course of such a training regime, over time athletes will experience a development in their aerobic potential. This means they will have developed their overall fitness base, and are better prepared physically for the season ahead. If a player is able to jog continuously for forty-five minutes then they are ready to start more intense exercise for that period, such as interval or speed training.

In essence, continuous training is just that:

continuous, meaning constant exercise at a stable intensity. On the training field this may be in the form of long, slow distance running, but it could be replicated in the gym on an exercise bike or in the pool with swimming. To prevent boredom, variety can be added to these runs by introducing balls and cones and getting the players to dribble between cones or around corner flags. As long as they are running in a continuous fashion and are able to talk, then anything can be included. Continuous training will help prepare the body to keep moving for certain periods of time, and once this has been established it will be able to adapt so this length of time can be filled with more strenuous activity.

Example 1: Long Steady Run

A long, steady run can be completed anywhere, and a regularly changing route will prevent the players from getting bored. This can be completed individually and away from the training session – thus coaches can give the players a distance to run or a time to run prior to the next training session. The length of the run could be based on each player's needs, and given that soccer is played in minutes and not by distance covered, it would be best measured by the number of minutes the players are active. Thus they might start with a thirty-minute run and develop this week by week and month by month to produce an overall increased aerobic potential.

Example 2: Pitch Endurance

Pitch endurance is all about getting the players to run continuously, and including a ball in order to raise the training stimulus. Using

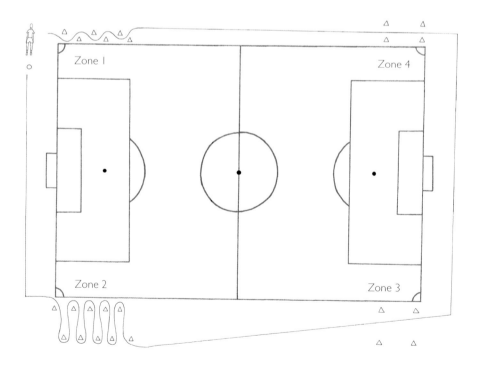

Fig. 23 Pitch endurance.

a pitch, or if available, a sports field with more than one pitch, players dribble a football around the pitch for the duration of the activity (as above dictated by the coach, but which should be progressive with a minimum of twenty minutes).

Players complete dribbling exercises set out with cones or slalom poles in each of zones 1 to 4 (Fig. 23). While the emphasis should be on continuous running and not dribbling, players should complete each exercise in order to keep them engaged in the activity and prevent boredom. In zone 1, players should dribble in and out of the cones on their way round the course. In zone 2 they should dribble round a red cone before dribbling round a blue cone, until they have dribbled round all the cones. Players then leave their balls in zones 2 and 4, and swap their ball with another player.

Coaches can vary this as they see fit, with other dribble-type exercises in each zone. The main focus is to get the players to run continuously for a pre-selected length of time.

Interval Training

Interval training differs from continuous training in that it consists of a series of exercise bouts interspersed with a recovery period. Interval training enables intensity to be high while the volume (the amount of work undertaken) of the training session can be extended. For example, if a player were asked to run at a high intensity for a prolonged period then the session would not last very long as the player would fatigue relatively quickly, and any adaptation to training would be minimal. Accordingly, a player might run at a high intensity for a given period of time (0.5s – five minutes),

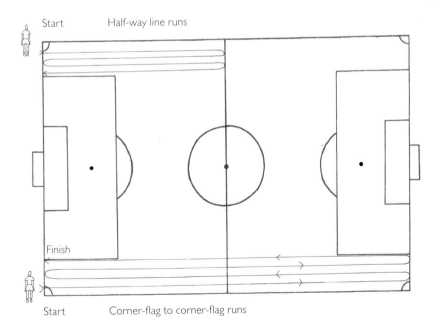

Fig. 24   Line running.

followed with a similar period of rest. This will enable him to make more training runs, and will give a greater opportunity for adaptation to the training to occur. The rest period prescribed is therefore important, and the period of work should be replicated by the period of rest in a work-to-rest ratio of 1:1.

Interval training can be utilized to develop both the aerobic and anaerobic training capacities of players, with aerobic work periods being longer, and anaerobic work periods being short, high intensity bouts of exercise. As this chapter is focusing on aerobic training, the examples below will focus on that.

It is worth noting that interval training, given its repetitive nature and high level of intensity, puts a great deal of stress on the body and accordingly should be managed carefully with players.

Example 1: Line Running

Line running uses the pitch and the lines of the pitch to mark out where the players are to run (Fig. 24). They start by the corner flag, and run to the half way line and back twice, then rest for the same amount of time. They complete this three times, then rest for three minutes. Once the rest time is over they repeat the exercise, but this time from the half way line to the corner flag, and again repeat this three times with associated rest periods after each attempt. Increasing the running distance can further develop the duration, players running from corner flag to corner flag and back. This should be repeated in the same way, with rest breaks in between repetitions. This should all be completed at a high intensity. A ball can be included here, but it is important that this does not sacrifice the intensity with which the players are running.

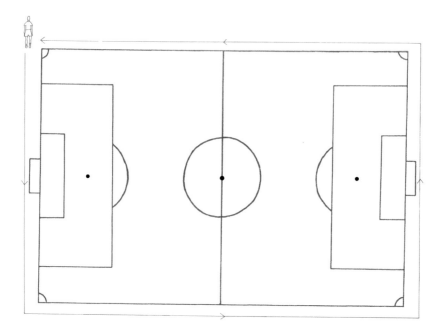

Fig. 25   Pitch running.

Example 2: Pitch Running

Players are set the challenge of seeing how many laps of the pitch they can complete in a three-minute period (Fig. 25). Upon completion they mark the distance they have covered with a cone, and enjoy a three-minute rest period. They then repeat this exercise to see if they can beat their previous distance. The coach should provide plenty of encouragement, and should try to keep the athletes motivated to beat their previous distance. The players should have four attempts at this, with recovery periods included after each.

Fartlek Training

Fartlek training was devised in Sweden by distance runners, and is loosely translated as 'speed play'. It is a combination of continuous and interval training, as it involves training at

a variety of intensities in one session, players alternating between fast, steady and slow running speeds.

Fartlek training is extremely adaptable and flexible, and as such can be applied to a variety of sports by mimicking match actions. The game of soccer often asks the player to perform different actions, but no player runs hard for the entire duration of the game, and there are periods of jogging and walking. Fartlek training can replicate the match demands, and so players can train for the game directly. Similarly, soccer is not all about running in a straight line and requires frequent changes of direction, sidestepping and running backwards. With Fartlek training this can again be replicated in the training programme for the players, to ensure that they practise moving at different intensities

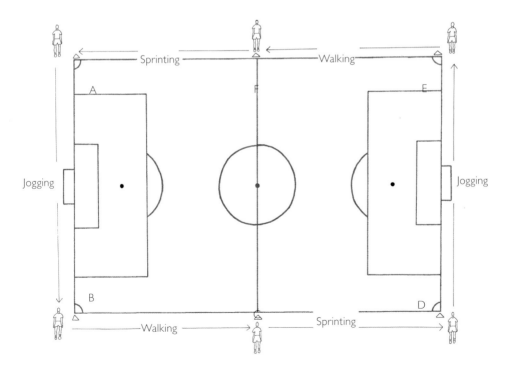

Fig. 26   Ready, steady, go.

49

and in different directions, as they might in a match.

Soccer, by its very nature, contains a multitude of movements that are varied and unpredictable, and with Fartlek training these sequences can be developed and trained for on the practice field. It is recommended that Fartlek training should last a minimum of twenty minutes so players can reap the maximum benefit from it, and develop their aerobic potential.

Example 1: Ready, Steady, Go

This exercise again makes use of the one thing that is constant in soccer: a pitch (Fig. 26). Ideally, every team should have access to a pitch for training, and it is the obvious tool to use. As previously highlighted, soccer consists of sprinting, walking and jogging, and in this exercise the players perform each of these actions. They start at cone A, and every time they reach a new cone they should change pace. As shown in Fig. 26, the sequence is from jogging to walking to sprinting, before returning to jogging and starting the sequence all over again. Players should do this exercise for twenty minutes, and in order to mimic the exact movements in a game the coach might stipulate that in the first lap the movement is forwards, in the second the players should side-step, and in the third they should move backwards. Alternatively they might work these movements between certain cones: for instance, they might jog backwards between cones D and E, and so on.

Example 2

This exercise is based away from a pitch and can be carried out in any environment – on a road or in woodland – and could be work that players are asked to do away from the training session. They should follow the sequence below, and could include varying movements and directions if they so wish; they should repeat the sequence four times:

- Jog for 60sec
- Run hard (75 per cent pace) for 90sec
- Jog for 45sec
- Sprint for 15sec
- Jog for 30sec
- Walk for 30sec
- Run backwards for 30sec
- Run hard for 60sec

Small-Sided Games

Small-sided games are a viable training methodology for enhancing soccer-specific fitness as they require the players to perform similar movements to that required in a full-blown game with the same pressures and physical exertions. Nothing can be more specific in terms of training than playing the game itself. Small-sided games are extremely flexible and adaptable, and by manipulating certain factors the focus of the game, and indeed the physiological stress placed upon the body, can be tailored to the goals of the session and the needs of the players. Coaches can change the pitch size, the number of players, match duration, rules and so on, in order to produce the required physiological adaptation. The possibilities are endless, given the variables that a coach is able to manipulate; below are just a couple of examples that could be used.

Example 1: One versus One Game

Mark out a 10 × 10 grid with cones and use two slalom poles to make goals at either end (as illustrated in Fig. 27). Players then play for four minutes, and the person with the most goals scored wins. Players should repeat this four to five times. The ideal situation would be to have a series of these games going on at once, so that following a rest period, players move to the next pitch and play against someone else for each of the repetitions.

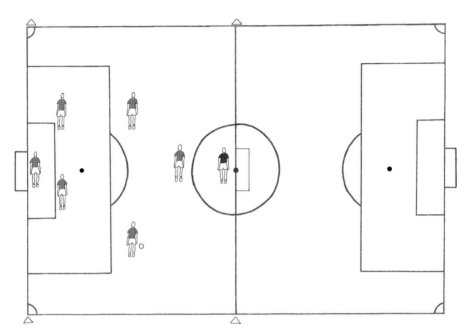

Fig. 27   One versus six game.

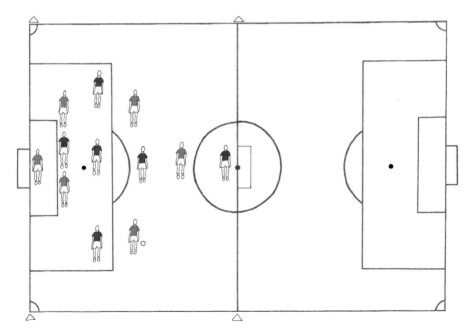

Fig. 28   Six versus six game.

There should also be a number of balls placed around the outside of the pitch so that the game can be continued and is not disrupted by stray footballs.

Example 2: Six versus Six Game
This game is played with twelve players (although this could be changed, depending on the number in the session), and on half the pitch (Fig. 28). A goal is required for both teams, and the team that scores the most after ten minutes wins. Following this game the teams should be revised and the game repeated.

A coach could devise variations on this theme, based on the overall needs of the group. He or she could insist on ten completed passes before a shot on goal, or could remove the goal altogether and make the game purely about retaining possession (for example, ten passes might equal one goal), if this were a particular need of the group. He or she could mark out the pitch with a half way line, and players could only shoot following a dribble across the half way mark, if the group needed to practise running with the ball more. There could be an overload (six against four) attacking if he or she considered the attacking element needed to be practised, or defending if he or she felt it was necessary to practise playing out from the back.

This is by no means an exhaustive list, and given the parameters that a coach can change, the possibilities really are endless. Remember that the focus is still on aerobic fitness, and the technical factors are a bi-product of this. It is important to ensure there are plenty of footballs close by so that the game is not interrupted, thus challenging the aerobic system.

Summary

Aerobic training forms an integral part of developing soccer fitness, and as such needs to be given attention both pre-season and in the season. The forms of aerobic training are all extremely flexible, and can be developed as the player or coach sees fit, as long as the primary focus throughout is on the development of the aerobic potential. Whilst it is beneficial to include the football in such activities along with different skill development exercises, this should not be allowed to detract from the quality of the activity: that is, the intensity and/or duration of the exercise should not be impacted.

It is important that the fundamentals of each training method are followed throughout. When used pre-season to develop aerobic capacity, the training methods listed above could be used in the order detailed, the continuous training coming at the start of pre-season sessions, the small-sided games coming closer to the season's start, with interval and Fartlek training in between. This is due to the fact that as the sequence moves away from continuous training, everything becomes more soccer specific. This is a suggestion and not a necessity, and coaches should develop their training plan based upon the players' needs, as in fitness training the objectives will always lead the methods.

CHAPTER 5

ANAEROBIC TRAINING FOR SOCCER

Anaerobic training prepares the body for the frequent bouts of high intensity activity that are performed throughout competition. The repeated sprint nature of soccer ensures that anaerobic training is a fundamental element of soccer fitness and an integral part of improving performance. Soccer contains a great many intense activities – sprinting, tackling, jumping, changing direction – that utilize the anaerobic energy pathway, and by undertaking anaerobic training, players are preparing themselves to be able to sprint, recover, and sprint again throughout an entire game.

Anaerobic training will help players improve their speed over the short sprints that typify soccer, and will also help them to develop the length of time each sprint can be sustained. These increases could mean the difference between being able to make that run into the penalty box in the ninetieth minute or not, between making the interception or not winning back possession of the ball, and between making that goal-line clearance or watching the ball cross the goal line.

This chapter retains the focus on the practical element of soccer fitness, yet the emphasis here moves to anaerobic training. The need for anaerobic training in soccer is discussed first, followed by a framework for establishing the dynamic movements associated with the game, before outlining training protocols that can be employed to develop the anaerobic aspect of a player's physiological system.

Improving Anaerobic Performance

Anaerobic performance is advanced by virtue of an improved efficiency and economy of movement, and by training each player's speed endurance. These exercises need to be undertaken at near maximal capacity to ensure that the anaerobic system is loaded sufficiently in order to lead to adaptation in the physiological state. In order to improve anaerobic performance, players need to be engaged in a programme of speed training and speed endurance training. Speed training helps players increase their speed through a combination of movement mechanics training and some sprint work. Once speed is developed and the quality of the movement established, speed endurance focuses on the improvement in anaerobic capacity – improving the length of time that sprints can be maintained, and the ability to recover quickly and sprint again.

Speed Training: Movement Mechanics

The development of movement mechanics is an integral part of developing anaerobic performance. After all, if a player were striking the ball with their toe rather than their laces, a coach would not focus on increasing the power of the strike until the player had the correct technique. This principle is replicated when looking to develop the players' anaerobic capacity. Each player needs to develop the correct movement technique first: once this has been established he or she can move on to repeating this technique in field-based practices, and eventually in the competitive environment. Well performed movement mechanics have a direct impact on overall speed, and can make the difference between getting away from the defender on the break, and scoring the goal or not. As has already been discussed, soccer is a multi-sprint activity involving a great many accelerations, decelerations and top speed running, interspersed with changes of direction in a variety of directions. Accordingly, when identifying movement mechanics appropriate to soccer, each of these needs to be considered.

When attempting to move quickly it is important that the arms are fully utilized. They will act as a counter-movement action to the legs in order to add balance, but will also drive the legs. The arm drive should follow the hip-to-lip guide, where the hand starts at the hip and drives through to the lip, with the elbow bent at 90 degrees throughout. The elbow should then drive the arm backwards to return the hand to the hip to complete the action. The hands should be relaxed, and the wrists should brush the pockets on the way past. These points should be applied for each of the phases detailed below.

Acceleration

When developing acceleration technique it is important to look at acceleration itself, as well as the starting position. An ineffective start will directly impact upon acceleration – if a 100m sprinter does not drive out of the blocks then they do not accelerate at the same rate as the other athletes, and so experience a poor start. It is the same principle in

soccer – if a player wants to be the first to the ball, then they need to get the best possible start and translate this power into the acceleration phase.

Fig. 29   Acceleration.

Players should lean their torso forwards from the upright position to a 45-degree angle before pushing off with the legs. Ideally they will have one leg in front of the other, with the front leg at 90 degrees. The back leg should produce a large amount of the force for the start, but should lift off before the front leg. The body will start in a low position and will rise as the acceleration phase develops. The torso should be leaning towards the target, with the head in front of the lead knee. Players should be encouraged to perform plenty of foot strikes/contacts in a short space of time – that is, they need to have a high stride frequency when accelerating. The whole body should be driving towards the same target – each limb should be working in a straight line and towards the target.

A common error made by soccer players is that their arms drive across their body and thus create a rotational force around their spine. This takes energy in another direction, and so the body needs to use some of its muscles to help stabilize this rotation, which means that its focus is no longer on maximal speed production. Whilst initially the stride frequency is high and consequently the stride length is short, these should gradually swap roles as the sprint progresses, so that as the stride frequency becomes lower, the stride length should increase, until the acceleration phase is complete.

Top Speed Running

Running at top speed is something that every soccer player does, but whether they do it as quickly as they could is another matter. Whilst a great deal of time is spent teaching young people the technical elements of a variety of sports, very little, if any, is spent teaching people how to run. Consequently there are many elements of top speed running performance that are not executed as well as they could be, which in turn has an impact on overall speed.

The head should be high and in line with the spine with the eyes looking forwards. The torso should be tall and relaxed throughout the movement. The feet should point directly ahead towards the target, and foot contacts should be made with the ball of the foot. Finally, the aim is to drive the leg forwards with a high knee action.

Deceleration

Decelerating quickly and effectively is often overlooked but could help lose the opposition when dribbling the ball, or help the defender stabilize him or herself and make a recovering tackle following a counter attack. The mechanics of this movement are also very similar to that of acceleration, where the player needs to make many foot strikes /contacts in a short space of time in order to slow down quickly and effectively. There should also be a slight lean backwards in the torso when decelerating, though it should only be gentle, with a minimal angle. The body position will be high early on as the player will have been running at top speed, but then as the body angle begins to decrease so should the height, ending up in a low position.

Fig. 31   Deceleration.

Fig. 30   Top speed running.

Running Backwards

Running backwards is only used for very short bursts in soccer, often when defending. Due to the bursts being very short in nature, it is vital that the player is as quick as possible so that they remain in position on the field of play. When running backwards the player should have a low body position with their chest high. Hips and shoulders should be square on, and they should not rotate when moving backwards (otherwise they would be wasting energy in a sideways direction). Arms will be used to drive as a counter movement

Fig. 32   Running backwards.

to the knees, and the player will exert a lot of force through their foot with a slight body lean towards their target (or along the line they are running).

Changing Direction at Speed

Being able to change direction quickly and efficiently is of importance both when in possession and when not in possession. This will help a player in possession of the ball to create an angle to execute a shot or cross away and out of possession to drive into that space to make an angle to receive the ball or lose a defender. The head should lead any

change in movement and should be outside the body in order to do this – if turning right, the head should be over to the right, outside the right leg. Both the head and a slight lean in the torso towards the target should represent the direction of the movement. The hips

Fig. 33   Changing direction at speed.

should remain square on during any changes of direction in order to produce a powerful movement. As with acceleration and deceleration, there should be very frequent foot strikes/contacts in the early phase of the movement in order to get up towards maximal speed.

Lateral Movement

Lateral movement has many similarities to the points discussed in 'Changing direction at speed' above, as both are about changing direction. Lateral movement mechanics bear many resemblances to acceleration technique, as moving sideways will still require the player to accelerate through the movement, but this time rather than the direction being forwards, it will be to the side. A soccer player will use this a great deal in defensive situations and when shadowing other players, so these movements need to be completed quickly so as not to give the opponents even the smallest opportunity to gain space.

The common misconception with lateral movement is that the player makes a high skip from one side to the other. Skipping like this should be avoided, however, because when the player is in the air between ground contacts the game situation could change quickly, and without any point of contact on the floor the player is unable to react to this change. Accordingly, players should be taught to adopt more of a shuffling technique, with one foot in contact with the ground at all

Fig. 34   Lateral movement.

times so they can react to any change of direction as required in the game. The head should be outside the frame of the body and leaning towards the target or in the direction of travel. There should also be a slight lean of the torso towards the target or direction of travel. The weight should be through the balls of the feet, and any lateral movement should be instigated through this area. The hips should remain square throughout the movement.

Speed Training: Stride Length and Stride Frequency

Speed is the result of the relationship between stride length and stride frequency. To be able to run at high speed, an appropriate balance must be found between both the frequency and the length of each stride employed. Stride frequency (sometimes referred to as 'turnover', or stride rate) is the number of strides you complete in a given amount of time: the more strides that are completed, the greater the distance covered. However, if the length of each stride is only small, then the overall distance covered – and thus the speed – will be low. Conversely, if a player has a long stride length then they are covering a greater distance with each stride – but if this causes them to have a low stride frequency, then again the player will not be very fast. Thus he or she needs to find the best combination of stride length and stride frequency in order to achieve his best speed potential.

To improve stride length the muscles that facilitate the movement need to become stronger, with increased flexibility around the joints: this can be achieved through speed resistance drills. An improved stride frequency will need a better developed neuromuscular system, and similarly this can be achieved through speed assistance drills.

Speed Resistance

Speed resistance training focuses on overloading the muscles and joints associated with speed performance; this will result in an improvement in explosive strength and stride length. The overload needs to be carefully managed, as it should not impact upon the movement mechanics, merely ask them to work a little harder. If the resistance applied is too great then the likelihood is that the player's movement mechanics will adapt to manage that extra weight, and the quality of the movement will be lost. In the long term this will result in a decrease in speed rather than an increase, therefore the overload should be applied conservatively. The resistance can come in a variety of forms, from loading the individual with weighted vests, weighted sleds, parachutes or harnesses, to using the environment and conducting some uphill running sessions. As long as the overload principle is followed and the mechanics are not inhibited, then there is scope to be creative when designing speed resistance drills.

Example 1: Sled Running

With the sled attached safely, the player runs twenty metres from cone A to cone B before resting for thirty seconds. He or she then runs from cone B to cone A with the sled attached, before resting for thirty seconds. Players should repeat this cycle twice before detaching the sled and running without resistance between cones A and B. The player should rest for two minutes, then repeat the whole exercise again.

Example 2: Uphill Running

Selecting an appropriate hill is of paramount importance in this exercise so that the overload does not cause the player to sacrifice running technique. The gradient should be relatively slight, 2 to 3 degrees being ample. Each player should run from cone A to cone B, with a gentle walk back to cone A; repeat

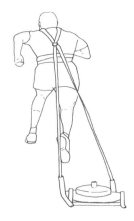

Fig. 36 Sled running.

this three times, then rest for two minutes. This should be completed twice.

Sprint Assistance

Including some form of assistance with the sprinting load has been proven to increase the stride frequency of a player. Essentially, speed assistance attempts to create an over-speed effect, which involves the player's limbs moving faster than they are accustomed to, and as a result advances are made in the neuromuscular system. Again the amount of assistance applied needs to be carefully considered so

Fig. 37 Uphill running.

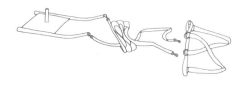

Fig. 35 Weighted sled.

as not to impact upon the running mechanics of the player, so this should be prescribed to each individual. The assistance can be in the form of harnesses, stretch cords, pulling systems and downhill running.

Example 1: Fast Feet Drills

This example makes use of ladders, but it could be repeated with anything used to mark the space in which the foot contact will happen – cones, coloured discs and hurdles are all viable alternatives. These are extremely flexible training aids and almost anything can be used as long as it meets the objective, which is to get the players to make foot contacts quicker than they normally do.

Fast feet drills.

Players should start at one end of the ladder and finish at the other. They should look to maintain the mechanics associated with running discussed earlier in this chapter, whilst moving through the ladder with an improved stride frequency. Players should go through the ladder ten times with a short recovery period between each repetition whilst walking back to the start of the ladder. Fig. 38 provides some demonstrations of ladder routines that can be used to improve stride frequency.

Fast feet drills.

Fast feet drills.

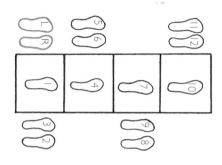

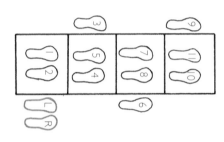

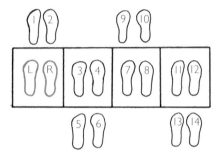

Fig. 38   Fast feet drills.

Example 2: Downhill Running

As with uphill running, the hill chosen needs to be carefully considered because if its gradient is too steep then the player will alter their running mechanics to deal with it; the body will adjust and the muscle actions will become eccentric in order to decelerate the body and maintain balance through the descent. Remember the overall objective is to get the limbs working slightly faster than they would normally, and a 2- to 3-degree gradient will offer that. Each player should run from cone A to cone B before a gentle walk back to cone A, repeating this three times before resting for 2 minutes. This should be completed twice.

Speed Endurance

Once the movement mechanics have been established and developed, training can move to focus on the improvement of the energy pathway. Speed endurance is the capability to produce maximum speed, and repeatedly achieve maximal accelerations and speeds as and when the game requires. As speed endurance covers the ability both to produce maximal speed and to repeatedly complete these sprints, the training is split into two sections: production training and tolerance training. Production training covers the devel-

Fig. 39   Downhill running.

opment of maximal speed, whereas tolerance training develops the ability to maintain speed over a course of maximal efforts. Whilst the same exercises can be used for each of these elements if so desired, the duration and work-to-rest ratios differ. Both should be completed at near maximal capacity and are relatively short in length.

Production training is anything from 20 to 40 seconds in duration, with the work-to-rest ratio weighted heavily in favour of rest. As these are near maximal efforts, the rest period for production training needs to be four to five times the duration of the effort: if the work duration were 20 seconds, then the rest time would be 80 to 100 seconds. The suggested number of repetitions of an exercise is six to eight.

Tolerance training, on the other hand, is slightly longer in duration, between 30 and 90 seconds, but this time the recovery period is decreased. The rest time is the same length as the duration of the work (30 to 90 seconds). The number of repetitions suggested is similar to those prescribed for production training, but this time they can be split into two sets, where the player will complete four repetitions before a rest, prior to completing another four.

Example 1: Pass and Shoot

This example is aimed at production training. The player works for around 20 seconds, and follows that with 80 seconds of rest; the exercise is repeated eight times in total. A goalkeeper and feeder are required for this task. The player starts in zone A by passing a ball to the feeder. Player A then runs round cones B and C before receiving the ball from the feeder and shooting at goal with their right foot. As soon as the shot is taken, the player runs to cone D, picks up another football and passes it to the feeder again. The player then runs round cones C and B before receiving

the ball from the feeder and shooting with their left foot. The player then rests for the designated amount of time before starting the second repetition.

Example 2: Soccer Endurance

This example has been written as if it were focusing on tolerance training, but it could easily be applied to production training with slight modification. Two players are needed to do this exercise, one to do the work and one used as a feeder. The player works between the lettered cones (starting at cone A and finishing at cone J), and the feeder moves along the numbered cones as the player progresses through the drill. The player must complete four laps of the exercise before swapping roles with the feeder.

The player starts at cone A and sprints out to cone B. On reaching cone B the feeder passes the player a ball. As the player will be completing the course four times they will perform a different action with the ball on each lap in order to keep motivated. On lap one they will receive the ball to the feet and pass it back to the feeder, on lap two they will jump up and head the ball back to the feeder, on lap three they will cushion a high ball on their thigh before volleying the ball back, and finally, on lap four the feeder will choose any one of the previous three actions for the player to complete.

Once the pass has been made, the player backpedals at a gentle pace to cone C, then sprints to cone D where again they receive and pass the football. They then backpedal to cone E and sprint to cone F. They continue in the same manner until they reach cone J, which marks the completion of one lap. The player then moves to cone A to start their second lap, and continues until they have completed four laps of the course. They then swap roles with the feeder (which becomes their rest time), and complete a second set of four laps.

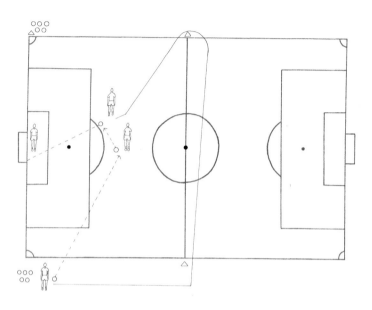

Fig. 40   Pass and shoot.

Interval Training and Fartlek Runs

Interval training and Fartlek runs are also viable methods for increasing anaerobic endurance. These are discussed in the previous chapter as an appropriate method for enhancing aerobic endurance, so they will not be covered here. The difference between the two is that any training exercises designed for the anaerobic system should be based around shorter work durations with higher intensities accompanied by longer rest periods than aerobic training, as developments within this system are all about short, sharp bursts of energy.

Summary

Anaerobic training is closely matched to the demands of the game of soccer. It focuses on the development of speed, and the ability to reproduce this speed time and time again. Given that this type of training is conducted at near maximal capacity, it is not always one favoured by players. With such a high intensity, it requires a lot of work from the players – but if they continue to put in the hard work, then the benefits are there, and they can train specifically for the movements and demands of soccer, which will in turn increase their performance level.

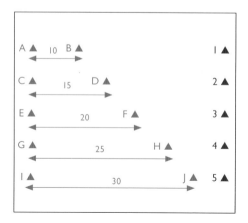

Fig. 41   Soccer endurance.

CHAPTER 6

STRENGTH AND POWER TRAINING FOR SOCCER

This chapter focuses on the development of strength and power in soccer players. It discusses the fundamentals of strength and power, as well as providing a rationale for including both into your training. Resistance training and plyometric training are then outlined in depth, including a range of exercises with descriptions, photos and illustrations to help you apply these types of exercise into your own training programme.

Strength and Power

The difference between success and failure in soccer is often down to the smallest variation. These variations can be due to any of the factors that are involved in performance. One such factor is physical fitness, which is one of the most influential and changeable elements of performance. This is an important point in the competitive world of sport, as performers are always seeking to gain an advantage over their opponents. With physical factors being amongst the most changeable, it is imperative that physical fitness and the training of this element are therefore given appropriate consideration. As a result, when planning any training programme, a coach must think about both maintaining and increasing the performers' levels of fitness, and the most productive and efficient method of doing so.

Power is a combination of speed and strength, and is crucial for success in many sporting events, including soccer. Due to the significance of explosive movements in the modern game, power has been described as one of the most important factors in performance – and being able to produce these movements in as short a time as possible is extremely valuable. Power is the ability to exert high levels of force, via muscular contractions, in the quickest possible time. The more quickly a muscle is able to exert maximal force, the greater the power output: this could get the player above his defender when jumping for a corner, whereas strength can help him win that tackle.

Strength is the ability to generate force against a load, and the production of strength, and thus strength training, is crucial in developing power. It is important to note that when training for strength and power it is essential to follow the principles of training as outlined in Chapter 3 to produce the most effective adaptations to the body.

Resistance Training

Resistance training improves strength by making the muscle work against resistance. This resistance normally comes in the form of weights, but it can also take the form of bodyweight. Intensity is measured by the number of repetitions (the number of complete movements) and the number of sets (a group of consecutive repetitions) completed by the player. The suggested number of repetitions for a strength programme is five to eight, with two to three sets. There should be an allocated recovery time between each set of three to five minutes, and the weight of each should be at around 85 per cent of a player's one repetition maximum (IRM). For power training programmes the suggested number of repetitions is lower, at one to three, at 80 to 90 per cent of his IRM for two to four sets. This should be interspersed with five to eight minutes of recovery time.

Below is a range of exercises that can be used to aid strength and power development. These should be prescribed based upon the athlete's needs and should take into consideration each of the principles of training outlined in Chapter 3.

Lower Body Exercises

Back Squat

This exercise works the gluteals, hamstrings and quadriceps. With the barbell resting across the trapezius, grip the bar with the elbows back. Start in an upright position, push the chest out, squeeze the shoulder

Back squat bottom position.

blades together and keep the head up. The feet should be shoulder-width apart and pointing slightly outwards. Ensure the back stays straight throughout the movement. In a controlled manner, lower the hips to the floor as if you were about to sit down, with the weight going through the heels. At the bottom end of the movement the hips should break parallel with the ground; then return to the starting position.

Front Squat

This movement is the same as the back squat, with the exception that the barbell rests on the upper chest (as illustrated). The exercise still works the gluteals, hamstrings and quadriceps, but with the different bar posi-

Back squat start position.

Front squat start position.

Front squat bottom position.

of the movement will also work the trapezius, backs and abdominals. The player should start

Deadlift start position.

Deadlift middle position.

tion, more load is placed on the quadriceps. Start in the upright position, and maintaining a neutral back position, lower the hips to the floor. The weight should be through the heels of the foot with the thighs breaking parallel with the floor.

Deadlift

The exercise will focus on the gluteals, quadriceps and hamstrings, but due to the nature

the movement in a squat-like position, with the hips below the shoulders. The bar should be against the shinbone, with the knees over-

Deadlift finish position.

With the barbell resting on the trapezius and the feet slightly apart, step forward. The torso should remain as straight as possible, with the head up, and the front thigh should be parallel to the floor. Gently push back from the lead leg to return to the starting position. Ensure this movement is controlled throughout.

Forward lunge step out.

hanging the bar. The feet should be between hip-width and shoulder-width apart. Squeeze the shoulder blades together and keep the head up. The hands should grip the bar with the arms outside the knees. Slowly extend the knees and hips, maintaining the angle of the back to the floor, until bar passes the knees (this will ensure that the knees and hips rise at the same speed, and that one is not loaded more than another). As the bar rises, bring the hips forwards so that the body is in an upright position to complete the movement.

Forward Lunge

The forward lunge will work the gluteals, quadriceps and hamstrings, but will also work the hip flexors of the trailing leg and the calf of the lead leg. The forward lunge can be executed with either a big step forwards (as illustrated), or a small step. A large step will predominantly work the gluteals, and a small step will predominantly work the quadriceps.

Forward lunge bottom position.

Side Lunge

Similar in nature to the forward lunge, the side lunge mimics the movement of a forward lunge but in a lateral direction rather than forward.

Stiff-legged deadlift start position.

Side lunge step out.

Side lunge bottom position.

Stiff-legged deadlift bottom position.

This will ensure that the groins (adductors and abductor) are worked, in addition to those listed for the forward lunge.

Stiff-legged Deadlift

The stiff-legged deadlift works the gluteals, hamstrings and the back (the erector spinae).

Starting in an upright position with the bar on the thighs, slowly lower the bar to the floor. The back should remain straight throughout, and the head should continue to look forward. The bar should stay close to the shins, and should not touch the floor.

Good Mornings

Like the stiff-legged deadlift, good mornings will work the gluteals, hamstrings and the back (erector spinae). From an upright posi-

Good mornings start position.

Good mornings bottom position.

tion (with a slight bend in the knees) with the bar resting on the trapezius and the shoulders back, slowly lower the chest to the floor

whilst pushing the buttocks backwards. The head should remain upright and the back straight throughout. Return to the starting position to complete the movement.

Step-ups

The main muscles worked here are the gluteals, quadriceps and hamstrings. Start

Step-ups start position.

Step-ups step.

Step-ups finish position.

Calf raises start position.

with the barbell resting on the trapezius, with the chest pushed forward, the shoulder blades squeezed together and the head up: then step one leg up on to the box. Ensure the knee is bent at 90 degrees before pushing through the lead foot to move the body up and on to the box. The torso should remain upright throughout the movement.

Calf Raises

As the name suggests, this exercise is designed to work the calf muscles. The player will need a small step in front of him in order to complete this exercise. Rest the barbell across the trapezius and stand in an upright position. With the balls of the feet on the box, gently lower the heels to the floor whilst keeping the barbell level and the back straight. Do not let the heels come in contact with the ground. Then raise the heels up before returning to the starting position.

Calf raises raised position.

Seated Calf Raises

The movement here is exactly the same as the calf raises detailed previously, but this time the player should sit down with the balls of the feet resting on the step in front. Rather than using a barbell to load the exercise, players can place a weight on the knees. Knees should be bent at 90 degrees throughout the movement.

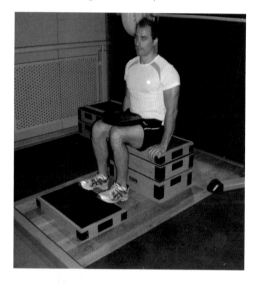

Seated calf raises start position.

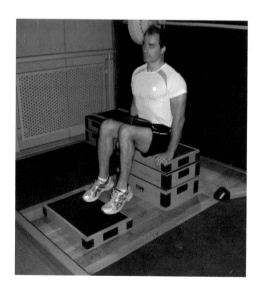

Seated calf raises raised position.

Upper Body Exercises

Overhead Press

The overhead press works the shoulders (anterior and medial deltoids), trapezius,

Overhead press start position.

Overhead press finish position front view.

Overhead press finish position side view.

Lateral raise start position.

Lateral raise finish position.

scapulae and triceps. This movement requires the player to start in an upright position: as the weights are moved above the head, it is important to maintain a strong core position and a straight back throughout. As such, the weight selected here should be done so conservatively. The overhead press can also be conducted from a seated position (sitting upright against a bench) in order to support the back. Raise the bar above the head until the arms are extended, before lowering the bar back to the original position in a controlled manner.

Lateral Shoulder Raise

This exercise can be conducted with dumbbells or using weight discs (as illustrated). This movement works the shoulders, and as the movement is to the side, specifically works the medial deltoid. Stand with a straight back and the legs slightly apart. To start the arms hang next to the body with a weight in each hand. The raise the arms to the horizontal with the elbows slightly bent, before returning to the initial position.

Anterior Shoulder Raise

This is the same as the exercise detailed in the previous shoulder raise, but this time the movement is to the front rather than to the side. This means that the main muscle worked is the anterior deltoid. With weights in each hand and resting on the front of the thigh, raise the hands to the front until they reach eye level before returning to the initial position.

Posterior Shoulder Raise

The final derivative of the shoulder raise is the posterior shoulder raise. This means that the movement is in the backward direction and as such will work the posterior deltoid primarily.

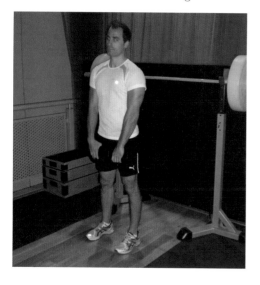

Anterior raise start position.

Posterior raise start position.

Anterior raise finish position.

Posterior raise finish position.

Lean forward at the waist and with a slight bend in the knees, keep the back straight with the head up. With elbows slightly bent, hang the arms down to the ground with a weight in each hand. Raise the arm to the horizontal position before lowering the weights back to the starting position.

Upright Row

The upright row is a multi-joint exercise and primarily works the deltoids and the trapezius. Start with the barbell resting on the

Upright row top position.

Upright row start position.

thighs with the hands just slightly wider than shoulder-width apart. As with most movements outlined here, the back should remain straight throughout this exercise. Pull the barbell up towards the chin whilst keeping the elbows high. Keep the head up, and lower the bar slowly until it reaches the original position. Ensure the barbell is moved in a smooth manner for the entire movement.

Bent-over Row

This exercise repeats the rowing movement from the upright row, but this time the movement is conducted whilst leaning forward from the hips at about 45 degrees. The move-

Bent-over row start position.

Press-up top position.

Bent-over row top position.

ment starts with the barbell just below the knees, and it is then raised upwards towards the chest, then lowered in a controlled manner to just below the knees to complete the movement.

Press-ups

Press-ups primarily work the chest and triceps. Lie face down on the floor with the hands a little more than shoulder-width apart, the elbows bent, the feet slightly apart and

the core tight. Push up to raise the body away from the ground until the arms are extended, before lowering the body back to the ground to complete the exercise.

Triceps Dip

As the name suggests, this exercise works the triceps. With the legs extended and placed in front of the body, place the hands on the edge of a bench. Bend the elbows to 90 degrees, then extend them to return to the original position. Keep the back straight throughout the movement.

Press-up start position.

Triceps dip start position.

Triceps dip bottom position.

tion for five seconds, and return them to the floor; repeat for the left leg and right arm.

Superman's raised position.

Core Exercises

Superman's
This exercise works the lower back. Lie face down on the floor with the arms and legs extended. Raise the right leg and left arm (as illustrated) from the ground, hold in this posi-

Dorsal Raises
Dorsal raises work to strengthen the lower back. Lie face down on the floor with the arms and legs extended. Raise the hands and chest upwards, and hold in this position for five seconds; then return both to the floor.

Superman's start position.

Dorsal raises.

Hip Bridge

Bridging at the hip will work the hamstrings, gluteals and the lower back. Lie on the back with the hands palm down on the floor along-

Hip bridge start position.

Hip bridge top position.

side the body. The feet should be flat and the knees bent. Push down through the feet to raise the buttocks from the ground. The hips should be raised until the knees are aligned with the shoulders.

V Sit-ups

This exercise focuses the abdominal muscles but does require a great deal of core strength and balance. Lie on the back with the arms and legs extended. Raise the arms and legs, and

V-sit start position.

bring them together to meet at the midline of the body. Keep the arms and legs straight, pause briefly when they meet, and then lower them to the ground.

V-sit top position.

Windscreen Wipers

Windscreen wipers is an advanced exercise, given the core strength and balance required to complete the movement, which works the abdominals and lower back. Lie on the back and raise the legs so that the hips are at 90 degrees and the legs are perpendicular to the ground. Keep the legs together and straight, and lower the feet as far to the left as possible.

Windscreen wipers start position.

Windscreen wipers right.

Ensure that the hips are angled at 90 degrees, and that the shoulders and upper back are in contact with the floor at all times. Return the feet to the upright position, then lower them to the other side.

Medicine Ball Twists

From a seated position, raise the feet from the ground and lean back slightly in order to balance on your bottom. The core should remain strong, and the back straight during

Med-ball twists start position.

Med-ball twist left.

this exercise. Holding a medicine ball in both hands and keeping your feet off the ground, rotate at the waist to the left and touch the medicine ball on the floor before returning it to the midline position, and then rotating to the right side.

The Plank

The plank works the back and the abdominals, as it is necessary to contract the core in order to maintain this position. Start by lying face down on the floor with the elbows bent

Side plank.

Forward plank.

at 90 degrees, resting on the floor. Grasp the hands together under the eyes, with the legs extended and the feet slightly apart. Raise the hips away from the floor and hold in this position. The hips should be just below the height of the shoulders, and should form a straight line from the ankles to the shoulders.

Side Plank

Lie on the left side with the left elbow bent and in contact with the floor. The feet should be together, with the outside of the left foot in contact with the floor. Raise the hips until

they form a straight line from the ankle to the shoulder, and extend the right arm upright. Hold in this position; repeat for the right side of the body.

Plyometric Training

Plyometric exercise is primarily concerned with the development of muscles in order to generate power and explosiveness. It is made up of a variety of hopping, jumping and bounding movements or throwing drills, and aims to link speed and strength in order to produce power. This form of training allows muscles to reach maximum strength in as short a time as possible. Thus by following a plyometric training programme, a player's power and explosive ability will improve.

It is also reported that plyometric exercise not only improves performance, but reduces the risk of injury in competitive athletes, thus demonstrating its importance as a training regime. Research has shown that high levels of impact forces acting through the knee lead to an increased risk of tears in the anterior cruciate ligament (ACL) – and these are common in soccer. Plyometric exercise reduces the landing forces that lead to ACL tears, and so this type of training is vital in minimizing the risk of such injuries. However, in order to gain the most benefit from plyometric exercise, and to reduce the risk of injury, jumping and landing technique has to be rehearsed in order to distribute the landing forces effectively.

The exercises should be smooth, with the hips over the feet and the chest over the knees. Knees and toes should always be aligned in both jumping and landing phases, and when jumping it is important to push off from the balls of the feet and land on their flats. An effective landing will be a quiet one, as most of the landing forces have been disseminated through the body. A loud landing means that much of these forces have acted through the joints, muscles and connective tissue, which will potentially cause injury. The forces should be absorbed through the ankle, knee and hip by bending with the jump.

When prescribing a plyometric training programme, the coach needs to consider a number of factors. As plyometric exercises place a large amount of stress on muscles, joints and connective tissues, coaches need to prescribe these sorts of movements conservatively, as overtraining can lead to serious injury. The best method of managing how much work is done is by measuring the number of foot contacts made by the performer: these should gradually increase as the player becomes more experienced with plyometric training. Beginners should complete eighty foot contacts in each session, whereas experienced plyometric practitioners should complete up to two hundred foot contacts a session.

As the performer becomes more experienced with plyometric training, not only does the number of foot contacts increase, but also the intensity of exercise. As demonstrated in the table 'Continuum of plyometric exercises', the exercise type can increase in

Continuum of Plyometric Exercises

Competence Level of Athlete	Exercise
Beginner	Sub-maximal jumps in place (short cone hops, ankle hops, split squat jumps)
	Sub-maximal jumps in place (tall cone hops)
	Squat jumps
Intermediate	Weighted jumps
	Low box and depth jumps
	Maximum jump without overhead reach
	Maximum jump with reach
	Tuck and pike jumps
	Depth jumps
Advanced	Single leg jumps

intensity as the players develop their technique and training history. So a newcomer to plyometric exercise would start with eighty foot contacts of sub-maximal jumps in place, whereas an advanced plyometric practitioner would work with two hundred foot contacts of the most intense exercises (depth jumps and single leg jumps).

For each of the exercises detailed in this section, it is important that the jumping and landing technique, previously mentioned, is followed. The description for each will not discuss the jumping and landing technique, but will describe the task for each exercise. This is by no means an exhaustive list, but merely an outline of exercises that align to differing levels of plyometric competence. Remember, the number of foot contacts and the complexity of the movement should be defined by their competence level.

Short Cone Hops

Set out ten short cones in a straight line, about half a metre apart. Players jump over each cone with their two feet together in a 'bunny hop'-like motion.

Tall Cone Hops

Set out ten tall cones in a straight line about half a metre apart. Players jump over each cone with their two feet together in a 'bunny hop'-like motion.

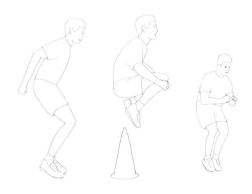

Fig. 43   Tall cone hops.

Squat Jumps

Place the hands on the head with the elbows out. The feet should be shoulder-width apart, and it is important to lower the hips

Fig. 42   Short cone hops.

to the ground whilst maintaining a straight back (getting into the bottom position of the squat). From this position drive up as high as possible through the hips, knees and ankles.

Fig. 44   Squat jumps.

Weighted Jumps

Weighted jumps are exactly the same as squat jumps, but must be completed with a weight. This can be in the form of a barbell across the trapezius, a weighted vest, or dumbbells held by the side of the body.

Fig. 45   Weighted jumps.

Depth Jumps

Depth jumps are performed from a height. Start on top of a box, then jump down to the floor and immediately jump as high as possible – the higher the height, the greater the training load.

Fig. 46   Depth jumps.

Maximum Jump without Overhead Reach

This jump is from a standing position: drop slightly, before jumping as high as possible. Keep the hands on the hips throughout the exercise.

Fig. 47   Maximum jump without reach.

Maximum Jump with Overhead Reach

This time the maximum jump can be conducted with the help of an arm swing to gain more height. As you drop slightly to prepare for the jump, rotate the arms backwards before driving them forwards and upwards to get as much height as possible.

Single Leg Jumps

Standing on one leg, jump as high as possible and land on the same leg.

Fig. 50   Single leg jumps.

Fig. 48   Maximum jump with reach.

Tuck Jump

Stand with the feet shoulder-width apart, the knees slightly bent, and with the arms at your sides. Drop slightly to prepare for the jump, then jump up and bring the knees up to the chest.

Summary

Both resistance and plyometric training can have a direct impact upon the overall fitness of the players, and as such should be utilized by coaches to help develop their athletes. Training for physical fitness is an important aspect in improving overall performance, but it does need to be carefully managed, well thought out, and constantly evaluated.

Fig. 49   Tuck jump.

CHAPTER 7

FITNESS TESTING IN SOCCER

Designing and administering objective tests for soccer players is important to measure the progress and effectiveness of any training programme. However, it is also necessary to establish baseline measures to create aims and targets to outline both short-term and long-term goals for annual training programmes. Training programmes are essential to prepare the individual and team to meet the demands of the game. Therefore it is vital that coaches are aware of how to test the current levels of fitness to produce a training programme relevant to the needs of the individual in order to achieve the required adaptations. It is common amongst many soccer teams to regularly assess the fitness of their players to identify whether adjustments to the training programme are required. The purpose of fitness assessments can be categorized into four key areas:

- To establish baseline data for individual players in the squad
- To identify individual strengths and areas for development
- To provide accurate feedback to players regarding their fitness levels
- To evaluate the effectiveness of training programmes

There is a range of laboratory-based fitness tests, which although accredited and extremely accurate, require specialist equipment and facilities. It is acknowledged that the majority of coaches and players do not have access to these particular facilities and would therefore benefit from more practical methods to implement into the context of their own coaching environment. For many years laboratory-based tests were deemed more accurate; however, in recent years certain field-based tests have been proven to be comparable to laboratory versions.

This chapter will therefore concentrate on demonstrating a range of practical field-based fitness tests available to all coaches to analyse the various components of fitness, providing accurate and relevant information on which to base training programmes accordingly. The tests will also allow coaches not only to implement these prior to planning their training programme to ensure the content is specific to the individual, but also to outline the importance of implementing the test throughout the annual training programme to monitor progression and development, and to assess whether or not the goals have been met.

The Role of Fitness Testing

Essentially, the role of fitness testing is to produce objective information for coaches, which will inform their practice. It is important that training is specific to the needs of the individual or team, therefore by obtaining objective information via fitness tests, valuable data will be provided that the coach can utilize, and which will help him or her to plan the train-

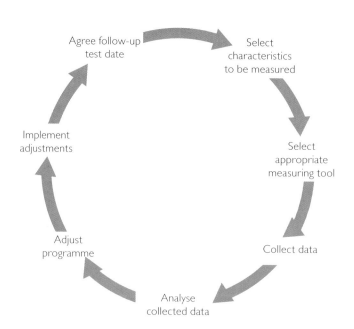

ing schedule accordingly. It is the information gathered from fitness testing that can inform his or her practice, and ensure that progress and development is being made in the correct areas. Fig. 51 identifies how fitness testing is a cyclical process, providing the coach with a standardized format that can be continuously applied.

There are many benefits of fitness testing for the coach. Testing can help identify strengths and weaknesses by providing an overall snapshot of the individual player's physical fitness. It can generate baseline information on which training programmes can be established, and can act as a monitor for over-training and fatigue. Monitoring player development is a key element in the success of training programmes, and by repeating fitness tests at appropriate intervals, the effectiveness of the training programme can be analysed. Results gained from the repeated tests will act as a motivational tool to drive players on to reach their goals, and will indicate when they have achieved their targets.

When working with a soccer squad there will be varying abilities and fitness levels, as well as positional differences. Fitness testing can enable the coach to group individuals accurately according to their ability, and to devise programmes that match their specific needs. Coaches are often faced with injured players throughout the season, and it can be difficult to know whether or not a player is ready to return to full training. Fitness testing can be used as a tool to help coaches make more informed decisions as to when to bring them back into training, and whether or not they are fully recovered from injury.

What Makes a Good Fitness Test?

In order for fitness testing to inform practice effectively, certain criteria must be fulfilled so that the information gathered can be utilized effectively by the coach. If these criteria are not achieved then the results produced may be misleading, and actually detrimental for player development. Therefore fitness testing must adhere to the following criteria: specificity, validity, reliability, accuracy and sensitivity.

Specificity

One of the major challenges that coaches face when attempting to implement fitness testing is to ensure that the fitness test mimics the actual movements associated with the sport in order for the test to be relevant, and to measure the fitness components specific to the sport. For example, a treadmill would be appropriate to assess a runner's fitness, whereas a cycle ergometer would be more suitable for a cyclist. Soccer is slightly more complex as it involves a range of movements and fitness components, therefore a range of fitness tests should be utilized so as to enable a true representation. Tests devised to assess fitness components in soccer should aim to incorporate the types of multi-directional movements and the distances associated with the sport. Test protocols should consider the specific muscle groups utilized, also the intensity and duration of the activity, and the predominant energy systems recruited.

Validity

In order for a test to be classified as valid, it must essentially assess what it is intending to test. For example, simply completing as many press-ups as possible may be a good measure of muscular endurance, but it is not a valid measure of maximal strength. This example would apply in soccer in the sense that if the fitness test lacked soccer-specific movements, then it is unlikely to be a valid test for soccer. Poor validity may also be evident if other factors have the potential to mask what is being assessed. For example, if testing sprint-ing speed in soccer, it would be inappropriate to require the player to dribble the ball whilst completing the test as this would be assessing dribbling speed, not sprinting speed.

Reliability

Reliability relates to how repeatable and consistent a test is. In theory, if a fitness test claims to be reliable, then if a performer repeated the same test under identical conditions with no change in their fitness, they should produce the same results. However, in reality it is very unlikely that identical results will be attained as there will be slight differences in the performer from day to day, with many variables to consider such as previous training, diet, recovery, fatigue and so on. Therefore coaches and players need to be aware that a relatively small change in test scores may not necessarily indicate any change in fitness levels, and the progression of players' fitness is not to be confused with minor fluctuations in test scores, which are most likely to be insignificant. This is an important consideration for coaches, because administering tests at specific intervals throughout the season is crucial in evaluating the effectiveness of training programmes, and in assessing the development of players.

Accuracy

Accuracy is relatively straightforward and is related to validity and reliability. Accuracy refers to how measurements are recorded. For example, if a coach were administering a fitness test in which it was required to time the test manually using a stopwatch, a highly skilled coach might be able to hand-time with accuracy to the nearest +/- 0.1sec, but would not be able to record accurately to +/- 0.01sec. In this, the concept of precision is also linked to accuracy with regard to the measurement taken.

It is important to be consistent when recording results. For example, a 20m sprint should be measured to the nearest hundredth of a second (0.01sec), and not to the nearest second.

Sensitivity

A test must be sufficiently sensitive to detect changes in fitness, otherwise there is a risk that the hard-earned fitness gains may go undetected. The sensitivity of the test is very much linked to how easily the test can be reproduced, with regard to individual differences as well as several other factors. Thus it can be extremely demotivating for performers not to reach their goals despite working hard in training – and it can be even more demotivating to acknowledge that there may have been improvements, but the test was not able to detect such changes: this will significantly undermine the credibility of the coach.

Field-Based Fitness Tests

The following field-based fitness tests have been selected because they are relevant to the movement patterns and fitness components associated with soccer. These tests are also linked very closely to the physical demands of soccer, as well as being practical to administer in any coaching environment. These tests are beneficial in that they adhere to all the previously mentioned criteria of what constitutes a good fitness test, as well as being safe and easy to administer to individuals, teams and large groups.

Vertical Jump

The vertical jump test is designed to assess lower body peak power explosiveness. This component is crucial in soccer for such actions as when a player is jumping for a header or making a tackle, or a goal keeper is jumping to catch a cross.

Equipment

A measuring tape and chalk, and a wall or a flat surface will be required to conduct this test effectively.

Set-up

Ensure that the test is conducted on a flat, hard surface. When using the wall-marking method, the tape should be firmly fixed to the wall.

Protocol

Players will first be required to remove their boots before testing starts, to prevent any height advantage, and before the actual jump the coach will record each player's standing reach height. For this the player must stand with one arm fully extended up the surface; however, it is important that the shoulder of the extended arm is flush with the wall. The coach will then mark the point where the tips of the player's fingers can reach on the wall: this will be the baseline of the jump.

Once the first measurement has been taken, the player should stand with the feet parallel and shoulder-width apart. The coach will then instruct them to chalk their finger and jump as high as possible using a counter movement with their arms: starting from an upright standing position, they make a preliminary downward movement by flexing at the knees and hips, then immediately extend the knees and hips again to jump vertically up off the ground to generate the explosiveness of the movement. They must not run into the movement to generate momentum. At the highest possible point of their jump they must touch the tape measure attached to the wall. See Fig. 52 for a visual representation of how the jump should be conducted.

Measuring the Test Achievement

Each player is allowed two jump attempts, and both measurements are recorded to the

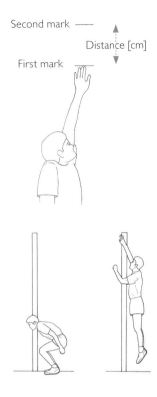

Second mark

Distance [cm]

First mark

Fig. 52   Vertical jump test.

nearest centimetre. The best jump height is calculated by subtracting the player's standing reach height from the highest score out of the two where they touched the wall whilst jumping.

Disqualification
The results are considered to be not valid if the following occurs during a trial:

- the athlete steps into the jump to generate momentum
- they bend or tuck up their legs while in the air
- the coach or whoever is administering the test cannot identify exactly where the athlete touched the wall

The 20m Sprint Test
The 20m sprint test is designed purely to test the linear speed explosiveness. This component is related to all aspects of soccer, whether that is making a surging run forwards to receive a pass, applying pressure to an opponent, or tracking an opponent to intercept a pass. Speed is essential to soccer, especially when playing at the highest level.

Equipment
Cones and a measuring tape will be required to mark out the 20m sprinting lane. Preferably electronic timing gates would be used to ensure accurate timing, however coaches may not have access to these, therefore hand-timed sprints are acceptable using a stopwatch.

Set-up
The test should be conducted on grass or artificial turf ensuring a flat, level surface offering secure footing. An unobstructed sprint lane of 20m should be marked out with cones, in addition to approximately 6m of recovery area laid out after the finish line.

Protocol
If opting for a stopwatch to record timings, the athlete should begin on the start line in a two-point (standing) athletic stance with the feet staggered. If using electronic speed gates, the player should start from a line marked 50cm behind the timing beam so as to minimize the chances of accidentally breaking the beam prematurely due to arm swing. The coach should instruct the player to start when they are ready, and to run maximally until they have fully passed the 20m finish line.

The coach should be aware that hand-timing begins promptly on the player's first forward movement from the set position, and stops once the player's torso crosses the finish line. Similar to the vertical jump test,

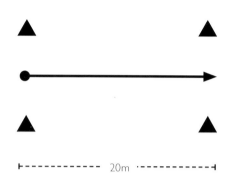

Fig. 53   20m sprint test.

two timed trials will be allowed; the fastest time can be used as the test result. Fig. 53 provides a visual representation of how to set up and conduct the 20m sprint test.

Measuring the Test Achievement

Each player is allowed two timed trials, and both measurements will be recorded to the second decimal point (the nearest [1/100]sec) – for example, 3.21sec. The coach should also take note of the running surface (whether it is grass or artificial pitch) and the timing method used (whether hand-timed, or using electronic timing gates). This is important, because when running a re-test later in the season, the methods used should be the same so that the test is reproduced consistently.

Disqualification

The results are considered not valid if the following occurs during a trial:

- the player makes a false start – that is, starts without first being set for 2 to 3sec, or uses a rolling start
- they start the sprint in a three-point or four-point stance, with the hand(s) down on the line

- they start the sprint with the foot across the start line (or across the 20in/50cm set-back line if the start is electronic)
- there is a timing error or equipment malfunction that prevents accurate timing, or casts doubt on the accuracy of the reported time

The Arrowhead Agility Test

The arrowhead agility test assesses the ability of a player to change direction at speed, as well as his or her body control. Soccer consists of many multi-directional movements such as dribbling towards defenders attempting to force them in one direction whilst quickly man-oeuvring in the opposite direction. The ability to change direction at speed is extremely useful in soccer, whether to outwit an opponent or to react to situations all over the pitch, and the arrowhead ability test will give the coach an indication as to which individual players may need further work in this area to improve this element of their game.

Equipment

Precisely six cones or flags will be required to mark all aspects of the course: the start, finish, centre, apex, and left and right points. A measuring tape will also be required to place the cones accurately, as identified in Fig. 54. As discussed previously in the 20m sprint test, either electronic speed gates or a hand-timed stopwatch can be used for this test, either one being acceptable. One important point to consider for the coach is to either tape or spray paint the centre point, as it is quite likely that the centre cone will get knocked and misplaced during this test due to the nature of the movement pattern. To maintain reliability the cone will need to be replaced at the exact centre point, if it is accidentally knocked, to ensure that all the distances remain as measured.

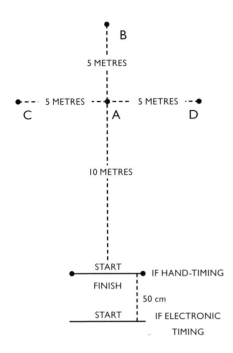

Fig. 54   Arrowhead agility course set-up.

are used, or a manual stopwatch. If hand-timing, the players should begin in a two-point (standing) athletic stance, with their feet staggered on the start/finish line. The coach will begin the hand-timing on the player's first forward movement, and will finish the timing once their full torso has crossed the finish line. Alternatively, if using electronic speed gates then the player will start 50cm behind the start line: as with the 20m sprint test, this will minimize the chances of accidental premature breaking of the beam due to arm swing. The coach will need to instruct the player to sprint maximally until fully past the finish line.

Running the Trial

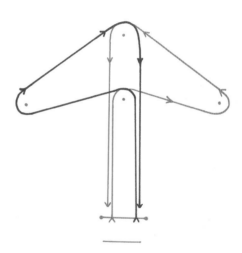

Fig. 55   Arrowhead agility course running direction.

Set-up

The test should be conducted on grass or artificial turf, ensuring a flat, level surface offering secure footing. An unobstructed course 12m wide by 15m long should be set up, plus an area of recovery beyond the start/finish line of approximately 5m. As can be seen from Fig. 54, the centre cone (A) is 10m directly ahead of the start/finish line, cone D is 5m and at 90 degrees to the right of cone A, cone B is 5m directly ahead of cone A, and cone C is 5m and at 90 degrees to the left of cone A.

Protocol

The arrowhead agility test requires the players to run the trial twice, once to the right side of the course, and the second to the left side (see Fig. 55). There are slight differences depending on whether electronic speed gates

The athlete lines up at the start/finish line for the trial to the right side of the course, and proceeds as follows:

- he or she sprints forwards to cone (A), goes round the left side of (A), and proceeds to cone (D)

- he/she goes round the right side of cone (D), and proceeds to cone (B)
- he/she goes round the right side of cone (B), and sprints across the start/finish line

He/she then lines up at the start/finish line for the trial to the left side of the course, and proceeds as follows:

- he/she sprints forwards to cone (A), goes round the right side of (A) and proceeds to cone (C)
- he/she goes round the left side of cone (C) and proceeds to cone (B)
- he/she goes round the left side of cone (B) and sprints across the start/finish line

Measuring the Test Achievement
Each player is required to complete one right-side trail and one left-side trial. The timing will be recorded to the second decimal point (the nearest [1/100] of a second) – for example, 8.57sec. The player's overall score will be the sum of both the right and left trial.

Disqualification
The results are considered not valid if the following occurs during a trial:

- the player fails to complete the course in the proper order
- they knock over a cone
- they step over a cone or fail to go round any cone or flag on the correct side
- they do not start in a set position and/or they use a running start
- there is a timing error or equipment malfunction

Yo-Yo Intermittent Recovery Test
The yo-yo intermittent recovery test (YIRT) aims to assess both aerobic and anaerobic energy systems in a way that is synonymous with the intermittent nature of soccer. The

YIRT is a great way to test the player's capacity to execute and recover from repeated bouts of high intensity exercise. Soccer is comprised of short, sharp, intermittent high intensity activity, which is evident in every single position, from goalkeeper to centre forward. Being able to perform and recover from these high intensity bouts continuously is integral to soccer performance. The YIRT is representative of match play activity, and will give the coach an insight into the recovery capacity and match-day fitness of the squad as a whole, and also as individuals.

There are two versions of the YIRT: YIRT 1 focuses on the capacity to carry out intermittent exercise, which leads to a maximal activation of the aerobic system; YIRT 2 determines an individual's ability to recover from repeated exercise with a high contribution from the anaerobic system. Both YIRT 1 and YIRT 2 utilize the same set-up and protocol, but there are distinct differences in the pacing of the audio cues, therefore requiring a different CD/audio file.

The YIRT is a 20m shuttle test with progressively increasing pace as dictated by beeps from the test CD or audio file. Athletes start out shuttling from one end of the marked course to the other at a relatively slow pace, and then quickly increase their speed according to the pace set by the beeps. Each bout of intense running (a 2 × 20m shuttle) is followed by 10sec of active recovery prior to the athlete resuming a sprint. The active recovery element of the test aims to replicate a break in match play in which players will be jogging back into position before their next bout of high intensity activity, such as creating space to receive a pass, or squeezing possession to put pressure on the opponent.

Equipment
The test will require cones, the exact number depending on the number of players the

coach is testing at one time, as the width of the area will be adjusted accordingly. A tape measure will also be needed to mark out a 20m shuttle zone and a 5m recovery zone. The YIRT requires the accompanying audio file or CD (either YIRT 1 or YIRT 2), which dictates the pace of the shuttles. The audio file can be easily downloaded from a range of sport fitness-related websites. A CD/audio player will also be needed to play the protocol at sufficient volume.

Set-up

The test should be conducted on grass or artificial turf, ensuring a flat, level surface and secure footing, either with individual players or as a whole squad – this is entirely up to the coach. However, when higher numbers are taking part in the test, players have been shown to give maximal effort and to actively encourage their teammates. See Fig. 56 for the course layout.

Protocol

The test is divided into several stages, each stage consisting of a pair of 20m runs (10m from the start/finish line to the outbound line, then 10m back to the start/finish line), followed by 10sec of active recovery. This consists of slow jogging in the recovery area, which aims to represent a break in match play when the player is tracking back into position. As the YIRT progresses, the amount of time that the player is given to complete each pair of runs gets shorter, so he/she will have to run at a quicker pace in order to maintain the required speed set by the audio cues. However, the 10sec of active recovery time between each pair of runs will remain constant throughout the protocol. Essentially the aim of the YIRT is to complete as many of the 20m runs as possible, whilst maintaining the required pace set by the audio cues.

The players will be instructed to start the protocol when they hear the word 'Go!'

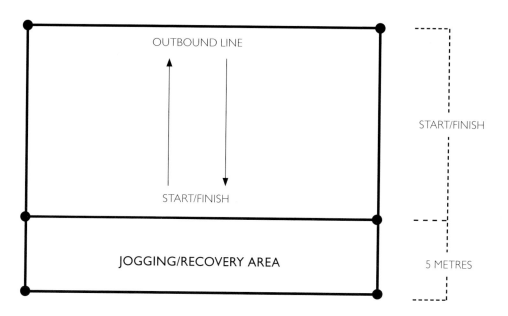

Fig. 56 Yo-yo intermittent recovery test.

followed by the first beep. They will then run to the outbound line – and it is important to mention that each player must touch the outbound line with their foot to ensure they are running the full distance, and thereby prevent disqualification. The second beep is an indication of the halfway stage of the 20m run in order to help the players with their required speed. Players should not stop at the outbound line when they hear the beep; furthermore the player is not required to reach the outbound line before the second beep – as previously mentioned, this is merely a pacing indicator, to ensure the player can gauge the necessary running speed.

The third beep indicates the time in which all players should have completed the 20m run and be past the start/finish line and into the recovery area. Players who do not reach the start/finish line before the third beep are assigned a warning; they can continue the YIRT with a single warning, but two warnings will lead to an automatic dismissal from the test. The YIRT begins at stage one, where the pace is relatively slow, however as mentioned this will become progressively faster, therefore it is important that players are aware of this so they can set their pace accordingly, allowing sufficient energy for the latter part of the test.

To recap, the instructions provided from the audio file will instruct the player:

- when to start running
- when they have reached the halfway point of each stage
- when the stage has ended, in which they must have completed their pair of runs and be over the start/finish line
- when the pace will increase on the next stage, and when to return to the start line after the 10sec recovery to begin the next stage

Measuring the Test Achievement

Depending on the number of the players completing the test, this will determine how many officials are required to effectively administer the test accurately. In general at least two officials are needed, however if you gauge it on approximately two officials for every ten players this will ensure all aspects of the monitoring and instruction are covered. One official will serve as the primary administrator in which they are responsible for offering instruction where needed, demonstrating the protocol, starting the CD/audio file and assigning warnings or dismissals. The second or third officials will be required to assist the lead administrator in identifying specific athletes who have been assigned a warning or who need to be given a dismissal. The officials may offer encouragement and motivation to the players during the shuttle runs to ensure players are giving their maximal effort.

The first time that a player fails to complete the 20m run by returning to the start/finish line before the third beep will receive a warning from the test administrator. As previously mentioned, each individual will be allowed a single warning, but a second warning will lead to automatic dismissal from the test. The test administrator will then record the last fully completed stage attained by that player, which will be their official score on the YIRT. Administrators and officials must take care to monitor the progression of the test, particularly the announced stages, to ensure the results are recorded with proper regard to the exact stage reached.

Disqualification

Warnings are administered if the following occurs:

- The players fail to keep pace with the audio cues (do not return to the start/finish before the third beep)

- If they use a running start at the beginning of any stage
- If a player fails to touch the outbound line with their foot

A player is disqualified in the following circumstances:

- if he/she receives two warnings
- if he/she voluntarily drops out of the test

Interpreting the Test Scores

All the tests discussed in this chapter are specific to movements associated with soccer and will help coaches monitor players' progress and development. Although it is important to administer each test effectively to ensure validity, reliability, accuracy and sensitivity, it is also important to understand the results of the test to be able to inform practice. For example, if a player attains a certain score on the arrowhead agility test, the coach needs to appreciate the context of the score to analyse whether or not the result is sufficient for that age or level of player. There are, of course, variations within scores between groups of similar age and level of performance, therefore the average scores presented are merely a guideline on which to base your assessment, and should not be seen as absolute.

STAGE	METRES	STAGE	METRES	STAGE	METRES	STAGE	METRES
1	40	24	960	47	1880	70	2880
2	80	25	1000	48	1920	71	2840
3	120	26	1040	49	1960	72	2880
4	160	27	1080	50	2000	73	2920
5	200	28	1120	51	2040	74	2960
6	240	29	1160	52	2080	75	3000
7	280	30	1200	53	2120	76	3040
8	320	31	1240	54	2160	77	3080
9	360	32	1280	55	2200	78	3120
10	400	33	1320	56	2240	79	3160
11	440	34	1360	57	2280	80	3200
12	480	35	1400	58	2320	81	3240
13	520	36	1440	59	2360	82	3280
14	560	37	1480	60	2400	83	3320
15	600	38	1520	61	2440	84	3360
16	640	39	1560	62	2480	85	3400
17	680	40	1600	63	2520	86	3440
18	720	41	1640	64	2560	87	3480
19	760	42	1680	65	2600	88	3520
20	800	43	1720	66	2640	89	3560
21	840	44	1760	67	2680	90	3600
22	880	45	1800	68	2720	91	3640
23	920	46	1840	69	2760		

Fig. 57   Yo-yo intermittent recovery test stages and distances covered.

Yo-Yo Intermittent Recovery Test Scores

There are many stages involved in the YIRT, and each stage represents the total distance in metres covered, as shown in Fig. 57.

The intensity of the YIRT progresses through the stages, making it increasingly difficult to sustain the required pace as determined by the audio cues. Therefore players with greater fitness levels will inevitably achieve a greater distance. Fig. 58 highlights the scores of male and female adult soccer players in a range of competition levels.

It is evident from Fig. 58 that the higher the level of competition, the greater the distance covered. It is clear that male top-elite players, who compete at the highest international level, had the superior performance, achieving on average 2,420m. Male moderate-elite, sub-elite and moderate-trained soccer players score an average of 2,190m, 2,030m, and 1,810m respectively. A similar pattern emerged in female soccer players,

again with top-elite players recording the highest distance of 1,600m in comparison to moderate-elite (1,360m) and sub-elite (1,160m). Research has also been conducted with adolescent players. Fig. 59 outlines the distance covered for both male and female adolescent soccer players. There is a prevalent increase in distance covered in both male and female soccer players throughout adolescence. This is an important consideration for coaches, as expectations of what results to anticipate from soccer players need to be relevant for their age and level of competition. Therefore although these average scores have been highlighted in Fig. 59, specific distances have not been detailed because these results have been given as a broad indicator, and not as scores on which to make direct comparisons.

Vertical Jump Test Scores

Lower-limb muscle power relative to body-weight is one of the crucial physical abilities

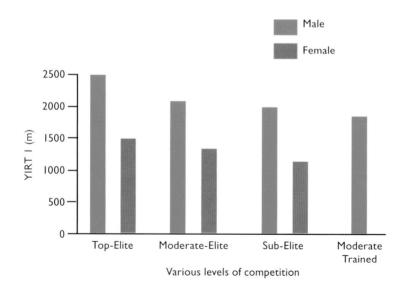

Fig. 58 Yo-yo intermittent recovery test scores for various levels of male and female adult soccer players. (Adapted from Bangsbo, Iaia and Krustrup 2008)

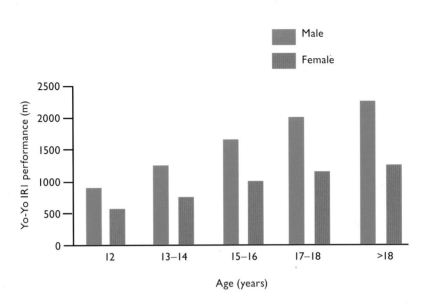

Fig. 59 Yo-Yo intermittent recovery test scores for male and female adolescent soccer players. (Adapted from Bangsbo, Iaia and Krustrup, 2008)

associated with soccer, therefore players who have this ability also have the advantage and will achieve higher scores in the vertical jump test. Research that has investigated jump height scores in athletes has found no significant differences between youth and adult soccer players. Fig. 60 highlights vertical jump average test scores from a range of adult athletes to demonstrate what is acknowledged as an above or below average score. Although studies have found no significant differences between youth and adult athletes, it is worth noting that there may still be slight differences; also these scores are taken from a range of athletes, and not solely those who are soccer-specific, therefore careful consideration is needed from a coach when comparing the scores of his own athletes.

Arrowhead Agility Test Scores

Multi-directional movements are essential to soccer, allowing players to change direction whilst still maintaining balance. The ability

Rating	Males (inches)	Males (cm)	Females (inches)	Females (cm)
Excellent	>28	>70	>24	>60
Very good	24–28	61–70	20–24	51–60
Above average	20–24	51–60	16–20	41–50
Average	16–20	41–50	12–16	31–40
Below average	12–16	31–40	8–12	21–30
Poor	8–12	21–30	4–8	11–20
Very poor	<8	<21	<4	<11

Fig. 60 Vertical jump test scores.

to conduct these multi-directional moves at speed is crucial to gain advantage over the opposition. Research has demonstrated that speed at completing the arrowhead agility test increases with age up to adulthood. This is due to the development of proprioception, balance, muscle coordination and motor skill. Average scores of 17.19sec for youth soccer players and 16.41sec for adult soccer players give an indication of targets for highly trained players.

20m Sprint Test Scores

Although straight-line speed is not seen to be as important as multi-directional speed in soccer, it is still a crucial physical attribute. A good score for highly trained youth soccer players has been shown to be approximately 3 to 6sec, compare to highly trained adult soccer players ranging from 2.8 to 4sec.

CHAPTER 8

DESIGNING A TRAINING PROGRAMME

In order to achieve success at any level in soccer, planning is a fundamental aspect of the coaching process, which cannot be overlooked. Effective planning is essential to the achievement and development of the coach and the team, but also – and perhaps most importantly – to each player as an individual.

As has been discussed in the previous chapters, there are many different factors that have a direct impact on how to plan effectively for soccer training, such as the principles of training, the predominant energy system utilized, and the particular component of fitness to be addressed. In order to be successful when planning a training programme a coach must consider and effectively combine each of these components to meet the unique demands of the specific coaching context.

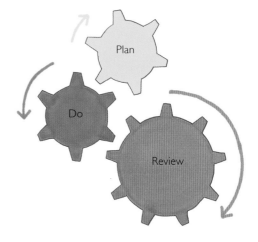

Fig. 61 Systematic coaching behaviour.

The Need for Systematic Planning

Perhaps the most fundamental requirement for the effective planning of a training programme is that it follows a systematic process, which is informed by the specific requirements of the situation, and is supported by systematic coaching behaviour. The latter should be used to help the systematic planning process by following the simple steps of the coaching process.

Plan: Set out a session that fulfils the aims and objectives of the coach and meets the needs of the players.

Do: Conduct the session allowing the players' development to dictate the speed of progression.

Review: Evaluate the session in terms of the development and understanding of the players and also that of the coach. Have the players achieved a satisfactory understanding of the learning outcomes/session aims?

It is the ongoing evaluation and analysis as a result of systematic coaching behaviour that is crucial in allowing systematic planning to occur. Without critical evaluation and ongoing reflection by the coach it is extremely difficult to develop and deliver effective training plans. Ensuring systematic planning is essential in allowing the coach to produce effective training plans which cater to the needs of the player(s) both as individuals and as a collective group.

For example, a coach designing a training programme for a team of twelve-year-old children who are playing their first competitive season together will have very different contextual requirements to those of a coach who is developing a programme for an international team about to compete in the European Championships.

However, whilst the context of the coaching situation will differ, the principles on which the training programmes are designed will be the same, and will be supported by the same systematic coaching behaviours, the only difference being the nature of the context in which the coach is operating. Thus regardless of contextual difference, the planning of effective training programmes needs to be developed systematically, and should be informed by systematic coaching behaviour.

When planning, a coach should observe the following criteria:

- Create a performance-enhancing environment appropriate to that of the player(s)
- Plan systematically to ensure organized and effective preparation and training
- Integrate all the necessary factors that affect performance into a training plan
- Divide the training year into a system of fluid and overlapping training periods that vary in their purpose, volume and intensity

- Relate each period to the stage of development of the player(s) and the occurrence of specific competition
- Incorporate the principles of periodization

Before designing a training programme it is essential that the coach develops an understanding of the players with whom they are going to be working. Training programmes must be designed as much as possible for the unique nature of the players and the team, and around the specific requirements of the individuals, based on their level of understanding and also their physical and psychological maturity and development. Although there are a number of theoretical principles that are fundamental to the design of a training programme, the key to success is to satisfy the fundamental requirements of the players to ensure success on the field as a team, but also for each player as an individual.

Establishing Goals

A fundamental element for any coach developing a training programme is to establish goals, both for themselves as the coach and for the collective group and the individual players in the team. Without goals it is extremely difficult for a coach to plan a training programme systematically, as clear aims and objectives must be established.

Through a process of effective goal-setting the coach is able to come to a better understanding of their players and to identify clearly the aspirations of the team. These aspirations provide the coach with a clear picture of what the players want to achieve, and it is then up to the coach to develop a training programme which contains the elements that enable the team to fulfil their goals.

To allow effective planning of a training programme it is crucial that the coach and the athletes are involved in the development of both team and individual goals. In order to be successful and to help the systematic planning process, goals should follow the criteria identified below, more easily remembered by the catch word SMARTER:

S: Goals must be **S**pecific, and the more specific the better. Each goal should be stated in as exact terms as possible.
M: Targets should be **M**easurable and assessed.
A: Goals should have **A**ccountability and be agreed by the participants and the coach.
R: Goals must be **R**ealistic and challenging but within the performer's capability.
T: Targets should be **T**ime-based: decide on a timeline for completion and stick to it.
E: Goals should be **E**xciting: exciting goals will be met far sooner than boring, uninspiring goals.
R: Goals should be **R**ecorded, in a place where they can be looked at every day – that way progress can be clearly tracked.

Established goals that meet the SMARTER criteria help the coach to plan an effective training programme by indicating the exact needs of the players within the specific coaching context. This allows the coach to produce the most effective training programme to meet the specific learning requirements of the team, which in turn allows them to achieve success in terms of both sporting performance and their individual and collective development.

Periodization

The concept of periodization is the foundation on which an effective training programme is built. It is concerned with the long-term planning of coaching sessions on at least a season-long scale to allow players to produce peak performances at predetermined points throughout the season(s). It divides the annual training programme into smaller training phases, which make it easier to plan and manage the training programme to ensure that peak performance is attained for the main competitions.

The fundamental principles of periodization support the development of both coach and player. For the player, periodization allows a structured training environment that is fundamentally supportive of technical and tactical development. For the coach, the principles of periodization demand the use of systematic coaching as a means of ensuring that the content of each coaching session, within the training programme, is informed by the outcomes and learning contained within the previous coaching session(s).

Periodization is also concerned with providing specific rest periods to ensure suitable recovery from the physical and mental strains of training through tapering. Tapering is the central component of periodization, which allows players to peak at predetermined points in the training programme, for example when playing an important fixture. Put simply, tapering allows players to replenish their energy stores and allows recovery through a reduction in training volume before or after specific competition. Not only is tapering an important element for achieving peak performance, it is also vital in the prevention of injuries, particularly those related to overuse. In order for tapering to be effective it is important that the intensity of exercise is maintained whilst the volume of exercise is reduced in parallel.

In order to facilitate systematic planning, periodic training is divided into three types of cycle: the macro cycle, the meso cycle and the micro cycle, each with its own aims and objectives.

The Macro Cycle

A macro cycle is a period of training that usually lasts one calendar year – although it can last up to four calendar years – in which a team or performer aims to produce a training effect leading to peak performance. The length and intensity of the peak will vary according to the sport and the stage of development of the performer/ team. A four-year macro cycle may occur when a team is preparing for an international tournament such as the World Cup. In order to produce a peak performance the macro cycle must be carefully structured, and should contain three basic elements:

- the preparation phase
- the competitive phase
- the recovery phase

Each of these phases can be used to periodize the macro cycle into smaller, more manageable meso cycles, as shown in Fig. 62.

The Preparation Phase

The aim of the preparation phase is to prepare the players fully for the demands of the competitive phase.

In any training programme and irrespective of length, this implies their general physical, technical, tactical and psychological preparation for the forthcoming competitive phase. This is exactly the case in the 'pre-season' phase of a training programme, during which the primary objective is for players to prepare both physically and mentally for the imminent competitive season.

In any training programme the preparation phase is essential in preparing players for the physical and mental demands contained in the competitive phase, and because it is during this phase that players make the most tangible advances in terms of physical and psychological development. If a player leaves the preparation phase without having achieved the required level of physical and psychological fitness, this will have a significant impact on their ability to perform well during the competitive season. Furthermore as a result of players not reaching the desired levels during the preparation phase, it is extremely difficult for the benefits of periodization to be achieved during the competitive phase.

To be most effective the preparation phase must be broken down into two specific sub-phases: the general preparation phase (GPP) and the specific preparation phase (SPP). These sub-phases need to be addressed as independent elements of the periodization process, each with its own aims and objectives, but which combine to fulfil the aims of the overall preparation period.

The General Preparation Phase (GPP)

The focus of the general preparation phase is to enhance the general physical conditioning of players across all fitness components required for soccer. The GPP occurs after players return from the 'off season' (recovery phase), and is used not only to prepare the players physically for the forthcoming season, but also to reintroduce players back into the psychological routines of the training environ-

Jan	Feb	Mar	Apr	May	Jun	Jul	Aug	Sep	Oct	Nov	Dec
	Comp			Recovery		Prep			Comp		
1	2	3	4	5	6	7	8	9	10	11	12

Fig. 62 Example of training phases in a soccer season.

ment. A very important aspect of the GPP is to begin to develop team spirit and team cohesion amongst existing players, and also to welcome any new members to the squad. The GPP is a good opportunity for players to reintroduce themselves gradually into the training environment, and to develop the fundamental fitness components on which the following season will be built.

One of the key aims for a coach during the GPP is to establish a baseline fitness level in every player in the squad, to allow more specific and skill-based adaptations to occur in the specific preparation phase. In order to achieve this level of fitness the principles of periodization are again important. To achieve the most successful GPP players should be expected to enter the GPP with a specific level of general physical fitness, achieved during the recovery or 'off-season' period from the previous season. This concept shows clearly the cyclical nature of planning an effective training programme, where every recovery phase in a training plan precedes and informs the following preparatory phase of the next seasons' plan.

A way of measuring a baseline of physical fitness is to utilize fitness testing at the start and end of the GPP to record levels of aerobic fitness in relation to the required baseline, and also to chart the progress of each individual member of the team throughout the training phase. Recording the results provides the coach with a clear picture as to the development of the physical fitness levels of the players in the squad, and allows the coach to adapt training accordingly to ensure that specific levels of fitness are met, thus allowing periodization to take place.

The Specific Preparation Phase (SPP)

The specific preparation phase follows on directly from the GPP. When players embark on the SPP, they should have established an accepted level of physical fitness across the range of performance components required for soccer. The SPP focuses on the fine-tuning of technical, tactical and psychological skills.

During the SPP, training is of a higher intensity and specialization than during the GPP. Whereas during the GPP players are likely to have trained as a squad, during the SPP they may begin to work in smaller groups based on the specializations of the playing positions in the team – thus goalkeepers/defenders/strikers may train separately, focusing on position-specific skills.

It is during the SSP that coaches can begin to focus on tactical and game-based training which is designed to test the players in match-specific situations. In order to be effective the SPP should contain training elements that are conducted at a high level of intensity, which begin to mirror those of the competitive phase. In doing so, coaches can identify the areas in performance which need to be addressed in order to achieve success in the competitive phase.

The primary aim of the SPP is to fine-tune competition-specific skills, and to prepare players for competition perhaps through the use of pre-season fixtures and training. Once players complete the SPP they should be physically and psychologically prepared for the demands of the competitive period.

When discussing the elements that combine to form the preparation phase, it is important to note that the GPP and SPP are not of equal duration, and it is up to the coach to determine how long the GPP (used to establish general fitness) and the SPP (used to fine-tune game-specific skills and tactics) need to be. This decision is based on a range of characteristics, including playing standard, ability, age, competition schedule and the predetermined goals of the team. For example, a team at the top of the Premier League (First Tier) may have a shorter GPP as they hope to use tactics and skill to win competitive fixtures. However, a team that has recently been promoted from the Championship (Second Tier) into the Premier League may have a longer GPP as a result of the fact that they may need to work at a higher intensity for longer periods in order to win competitive fixtures.

The way a coach decides to split the preparation phase is based on their fundamental understanding of the individual players with whom they are working, combined with their coaching philosophy and understanding of the competition level.

The Competitive Phase

The aim of the competitive phase is to maintain the gains of the preparation period, and to peak all aspects of performance for major competitions.

The primary aim of the competitive phase is to perfect training factors, allowing the players to improve their individual ability and compete with success in competition. Whilst focusing on the achievement of this primary objective, the competitive phase can also be designed to incorporate a large amount of technical and strength and conditioning training (if appropriate to the age of the players) alongside vital independent training; this is to allow the maintenance of fitness alongside the continuous development of skills and competitive manoeuvres.

During the competitive phase it is important that competitive fixtures are prioritized to allow the coach to specifically prepare the team to peak at predetermined points within the training plan. Once fixtures have been prioritized the coach can then ensure that appropriate training volumes and intensities are achieved in the micro cycles prior to competition, to allow players to be in peak physical and mental condition at predetermined points in the training programme.

There is a distinct need for the coach to adopt systematic coaching behaviours throughout the competitive phase in order to facilitate the effective periodization of training. As a result of fluctuating frequencies and intensity of training it is vital that the coach is able to inform future micro cycles based on the evaluation of previous training, therefore allowing fundamental areas for development and performance improvement to be identified.

It is also important to note that both physical and psychological fitness gains achieved in the preparation phase need to be maintained throughout the competitive phase; this can ,be monitored through regular testing of physical fitness alongside psychological profiling. It is important that testing and profiling are incorporated into a training programme to allow the collective and individual effects of periodization to be measured throughout the competitive phase. This information must then be used by the coach to inform future micro and macro cycles within the training programme, as a means of demonstrating systematic planning.

The Recovery Period

The aim of the recovery period is to recuperate mentally and physically from the demands of the competitive period.

The recovery phase is identified as the period from the last week of competitive training until the beginning of the preparatory phase of the following season in the training programme. The primary aim of the recovery phase is to allow the individual player to recover from the physiological and psychological stresses of the previous season. This recovery must be a controlled process: it is vital that the player maintains a healthy diet throughout the transition phase, as a fluctuation in body mass can prove extremely detrimental and can cause significant problems during the general preparation phase of the next preparatory phase.

The transition phase is designed to give the player rest with no direct intervention from the coach, although a light schedule may be advised for the player to complete. As the primary aim of the recovery phase is to remove CNS (central nervous system) fatigue, players should be encouraged to combine complete rest with active rest, including general enjoyment and physical involvement. It is crucial that the transition phase is a success as it provides a basis to the success of the forthcoming season's preparatory phase.

The Meso Cycle

Meso cycles are periods of between two and eight weeks which allow the coach to structure training in greater detail. Each meso cycle will prioritize different components of training based on its position in the macro cycle and the training phase in which it sits. Therefore meso cycles differ from each other in task, structure of contents, forms of training and training load. Each meso cycle should inform the next to allow systematic planning and to ensure that the most effective training programme is developed alongside the development and progression of the players. Meso cycles combine to fulfil the objectives of each specific training phase within the macro cycle.

When designing a training programme it is essential that training volume and intensity are considered throughout. In each meso cycle it is the variance in volume and intensity which determines the effectiveness of the training programme by allowing peaking and tapering to occur. This then allows players to produce the highest level of performance at predetermined times throughout the competitive phase. When planning meso cycles as part of the training programme, volume and intensity will fluctuate according to the phase of train-

ing and the position of the meso cycle in the annual plan.

For example, a meso cycle of four weeks at the end of the general preparation period may have a high volume of work carried out at a low intensity as the coach is working on general components of fitness and wants to develop aerobic fitness. Conversely, the first four-week meso cycle in the specific preparation phase may contain a comparatively lower volume of work but conducted at a higher intensity to replicate more closely the conditions of the competitive phase and to aid the development of anaerobic fitness.

The Micro Cycle

A micro cycle is a shorter period of time, usually lasting between seven and ten days. As a result of the short time-span, micro cycles contain very specific information concerning the frequency, intensity and duration of the exercise, to further support peaking and tapering. Micro cycles combine to fulfil the specific objectives of the appropriate meso cycle. Again, through on-going systematic coaching behaviours, each micro cycle should inform the next to allow training to be consistently aligned to the individual needs of the players in the squad.

An effective training programme should be broken down using macro, meso and micro cycles, as shown in Fig. 63.

When utilized successfully, periodization allows a structured and supported training programme of effective coaching for all players concerned. Nevertheless, in order to achieve the highest possible results, it is important for the coach to understand the individual requirements and ability levels of each player.

An important factor to consider when working with younger players in the 'initiation' stage of physical and technical development, is that more important than age is the rate at

						Macro 1					
Meso 1		Meso 2		Meso 3		Meso 4	Meso 5	Meso 6	Meso 7		Meso 8
Micro	Micro	Micro	Micro	Micro	Micro	Micro	Micro	Micro	Micro	Micro	Micro
1	2	3	4	5	6	7	8	9	10	11	12

Fig. 63   Example of a periodized training programme.

which each player is maturing. The maturation rate of players can determine not only physical capabilities but also psychological and technical development, information which the coach must appreciate when determining the frequency and intensity of exercise as part of an effective long-term plan to support the needs of each player.

The training components required in order for periodization and effective long-term planning to be successful are based on the principles of specialization and individualization. In order to achieve successful long-term periodized planning, it is important to follow the principles of specialization by incorporating both generalized and specialized phases of training.

When designing a training programme it is important that periodization is used as it ensures that sufficient amounts of rest and recovery are incorporated into training to allow players sufficient recovery from both the physical and mental strains of training and competition. It is important that periods of rest are factored into each phase of the training programme to facilitate the development and understanding of the players. If the required amount of recovery is not factored into a training programme then there is a serious risk of overtraining.

When a player is overtrained it can cause them to become 'burnt out' and physically or emotionally exhausted. Overtraining can be avoided, simply by following the training principles of periodization and individualization, ensuring a sound understanding of the unique characteristics of each player. The information obtained by adopting the principles of individualization can be utilized by the coach as a basis upon which to develop a systematic long-term coaching plan which has at its heart the welfare and positive long-term development of each player.

The following seven-stage plan effectively produces a periodized long-term coaching plan:

1. Establish general and individual ability levels within the coaching group, taking into account maturation rate and personal development to develop a specific understanding of how much training is required, the intensity required, and how often training is required.
2. Identify key dates within the season, such as first game, important matches, or breaks from play.
3. Construct a season-long plan which incorporates a range of generalized and specialized training encompassing a necessary amount of each.
4. Ensure that specific periods of rest are included prior to important games and/or tournaments in order to allow players time to suitably prepare and recover from the physical and mental strain of training.
5. Ensure that a broad range of soccer-specific topics is included in the plan to

ensure sufficient mastery and development of technique, skill and tactical awareness.

6. During periods of little competition such as 'pre-season', ensure that the necessary training components are focused on, to ensure suitable levels of preparation for key dates or times in the competitive season.

7. Incorporate suitable and regular fitness testing in the long-term plan to allow areas of particular progress or weakness to be identified and resolved.

By following each of the seven steps identified, a coach is able to ensure not only a broad syllabus of soccer coaching, but also a considerable contribution to both the long-term and continuous development of each player. The use of periodization and long-term planning allows not only gradual and structured progression, but aids the personal and professional development of the coach whilst supporting high levels of effective coaching.

The Practical Implications of Planning a Training Programme

When developing a training plan for soccer it is important to consider and incorporate the principles of periodization as they allow not only structured and progressive training but also have at their core the personal development and well-being of each player. The challenge for the coach in order to be effective is to gain a clear understanding of each player as an individual, and to understand the goals and aspirations of the collective group of players in the squad. Only once this information has been achieved can the coach begin to plan a truly effective training programme – that is, one which is effective for the specific individual and also for the collective needs of the players and the coach.

Finally, when developing and planning a training programme it is important to appreciate that the plan is not static and concrete; instead the concept of planning should be seen as a constantly evolving coaching aid which allows progress, and the effectiveness of training to be measured across a specified period of time. In order to be successful in developing a training programme it is vital that the coach is engaged in a process of continuous systematic planning which is informed by systematic coaching behaviour. It is this systematic approach from the coach which will allow a training programme to be most effective, and to evolve alongside the development of both the players and the coach.

CHAPTER 9

NUTRITION – AN ESSENTIAL GUIDE FOR SOCCER

The Importance of Nutrition

A good nutritional status is imperative to maintaining health; furthermore it is a critical factor to soccer performance. It has been suggested that other than factors such as training and hereditary limitations, optimizing nutritional intake is the single most important factor influencing athletic performance. Therefore optimizing a player's diet and consuming the correct nutrients should be regarded as a priority in all aspects of soccer, including before, during and after training and matches. The benefits of optimizing the diet are most prevalent during competition, when nutritional strategies help players perform at their best by reducing or delaying the onset of fatigue. However, the benefits of nutritional strategies on match days will not be as effective if nutritional intake is inadequate on a day-to-day basis. Optimal daily eating patterns enable players to achieve the platform from which they are ready to compete by supplying the necessary nutrients needed for adaptations to occur from training and to ensure the body is fully recovered after each session and match.

Every movement the body produces is fuelled by energy, which is provided from the breakdown of food and drink. As soccer players produce movement patterns that are much more frequent and at higher intensities than those typical of people who follow a more sedentary lifestyle, they need a well balanced diet in order to maximize and maintain their training requirements and achieve their ultimate potential on a match day. It is imperative that coaches and players are aware of basic nutritional principles to ensure that the correct nutrients are consumed for their level of training, whether that is to compete recreationally or at the elite level of soccer.

Nutrition refers to a process in which the nutrients derived from the consumption of food are broken down to provide the energy necessary for a number of functions – in the main keeping the body alive and healthy, and also to enable participation in physical activity. It is essential to consume a wide variety of nutrients, as no single food contains adequate quantities of each nutrient necessary for the body's requirements.

Nutrients are broadly broken down into macronutrients and micronutrients, as discussed below.

Macronutrients

Carbohydrate

Carbohydrate is derived from the diet in two main forms: as simple sugars and as complex carbohydrates. There is also a third type, fibre, which plays an essential role in the transport of food through the digestive system; however, fibre has a relatively limited contribution with regard to energy production for the body. Simple sugars can also be referred to as simple carbohydrates or fast-acting carbohydrates. These are naturally occurring sugars such as those found in honey and fruit, although they are also prevalent in processed foods. Clearly it is recommended that the majority of simple sugars are consumed from naturally occurring sugars as opposed to processed foods, which are also high in fat. Complex carbohydrates are found in both plant and animal sources, and provide a more sustained, prolonged energy release.

Carbohydrate is the preferred energy substrate of the muscles, and is necessary both to health and for participation in soccer, as every cell in the body uses carbohydrate for energy. In fact the human brain can only use carbohydrates for energy, so considering that soccer requires a vast number of decisions during each and every minute of the game, ensuring the brain has a sufficient supply of glucose is paramount for performance. It is necessary to understand the amount of carbohydrate we have in our body so that we can see the importance for soccer players of consuming carbohydrate.

There are three main sites in which carbohydrate is stored in the body: as glycogen in the skeletal muscle and liver, and as glucose in the blood. In theory the body has enough carbohydrate stores to fuel eighty to ninety minutes of continuous aerobic exercise, and five minutes of anaerobic exercise; however, the rate of glycogen usage is dictated by the intensity of the exercise. There may be occasions when soccer matches last longer than ninety minutes and involve more frequent bouts of anaerobic exercise, therefore if players have not consumed adequate amounts of carbohydrate in relation to the individual demands of training and match intensity, their performance would not be sustainable and might also result in injury, especially since carbohydrates are utilized in such general tasks as walking and sleeping. Furthermore, an inadequate consumption of carbohydrates would also have a continuing effect on the next day's training, as the body would not be able to fully replenish its glycogen stores.

Fig. 64 demonstrates the effects of a high and low carbohydrate diet on consecutive training days; notice the level of glycogen storage on day three as compared to day one. Although it is evident that even on a high carbohydrate diet it is difficult to fully replenish glycogen stores when training on consecutive days, the levels are still significantly higher than compared to a low carbohydrate diet.

As we have already established in Chapter 2, soccer is an intermittent sport. Therefore in order to produce energy to train or compete optimally we primarily use carbohydrate to do this both aerobically and anaerobically. Considering carbohydrate is the primary nutrient used to fuel exercise, and bearing in mind that the body has a limited capacity for storage, it is important that we consume adequate amounts to sustain training on consecutive days and to fully replenish the stores used for match days. Low body stores of carbohydrate can result in fatigue and impairment of performance, and can have negative effects on the immune system. Therefore sufficient ingestion of carbohydrate will replenish stores that have been decreased through exercise, and any excess carbohydrate consumed above the level that can be stored will be converted into fat and stored as adipose tissue. Furthermore carbohydrate, and specifically glucose, is the only fuel that the nervous system will use, so to ensure efficient functioning of the brain we need a sufficient intake of carbohydrate. The concentration of glucose is normally maintained at above 4mmol, so when it drops below 3mmol, the soccer player may become hypoglycaemic, which results in dizziness, weakness, hunger

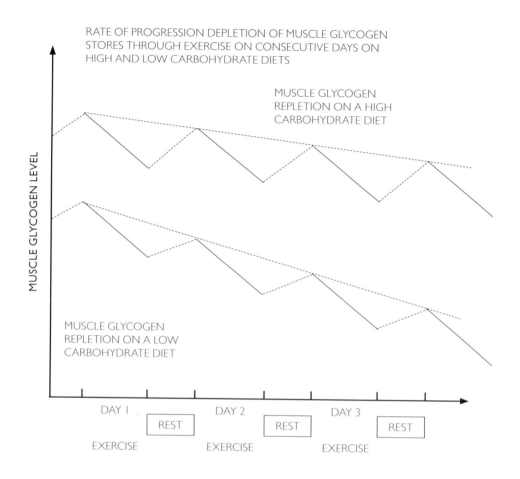

Fig. 64   Effects of a high and low carbohydrate diet on subsequent performance.

and shivering, and therefore has detrimental effects on health.

Fat
Fats are very important nutrients for the body, because not only can they act as a source of energy, they are also essential to synthesize important compounds and tissues which are vital for normal functioning. Furthermore, they act as a carriage for fat-soluble vitamins (vitamins A, D, E and K). Fats have a number of functions within the body, one of which

being a very good source of energy. Fats also provide thermal insulation in their storage form, as well as aiding in protecting vital organs such as the heart, liver, spleen, kidneys, brain and spinal cord. In the body 2–4 per cent of total body fat is stored round the vital organs, so if athletes have a lower percentage of this then it becomes dangerous to their health. Fats can generally be placed into two main categories: saturated and unsaturated fat. Saturated fats are normally found in animal fats, and high intakes can increase the risk of heart disease. However unsaturated fats can help reduce the risk of heart disease, and are the recommended type of fat to consume; they are generally found in vegetable and fish oils.

Fats are predominantly stored in adipose tissue, which is a type of connective tissue that contains cells of fat; most of these are located between the muscle and the skin. It is interesting to note that although carbohydrate is considered to be the predominant source of energy for soccer, fat can be stored in significantly greater amounts than carbohydrates. Stores of fat in the body account for approximately 80 per cent of the total energy stored in the body, with approximately 300g of fat stored in the muscle as intramuscular triacylglycerol. This is a directly accessibly store of fat for exercise, whereas the fat stored in adipose tissue has to be mobilized and transported to the muscle cell before it can be used to produce energy. This storage of fat would allow for over 4,000 minutes of continuous aerobic exercise, which far surpasses the amount required for any bout of soccer training or match.

This apparent abundance of stored energy prompts the question as to why do we need fat if in theory we have enough stored to fuel over 4,000 minutes of exercise – and furthermore, why do we need carbohydrate if this amount of fat is available? The answer to this is that fat can only be metabolized aerobically, so it can only fuel low intensity exercise, up to an intensity of approximately 60 per cent of VO2 max – and as already established, soccer requires players to work at greater percentages than this, at least for parts of competing and training. Fat metabolism therefore cannot be used to sustain high intensity exercise, which is why athletes need carbohydrate to sustain performance. Fat is still important, however, because when carbohydrate stores run out, then fat becomes the predominant fuel source for fuelling performance, albeit at a lesser intensity.

Protein

Protein differs from carbohydrate and fat with regard to the production of energy. Protein's contribution is relatively limited in terms of energy supply, except in extreme circumstances. Basically only if the body is starving, and when glycogen stores become completely depleted, will protein be used to produce energy for exercise. However, protein is essential in providing structure to all the cells in the human body, and to their growth and repair. Protein is also needed to support the repair of damaged body tissues, and the building of new proteins in response to the training stimulus. This need may be greater during the pre-season, for example, when a player is training heavily, or during a period when teams have matches with limited recovery time in between, as this kind of stress will lead to more damage of the protein structures within the muscle.

If we take pre-season as an example, and players are involved in resistance training, obviously one of the main goals of this type of training is to increase strength via hypertrophy, or by increasing muscle size. Hypertrophy is basically the growth of actin and myosin, the protein structures within the muscle. The training stimulus will provide some of this adaptation, but it is likely that after training, protein breakdown will exceed protein synthesis, so the growth of actin and myosin will be minimal. The adaptation will be considerably stronger with the intake of protein following training, as this will ensure protein synthesis exceeds breakdown, therefore enabling the growth of actin and myosin; this will allow for more cross bridges to be formed, and as a consequence more force production.

Current knowledge on the protein requirements of athletes is, however, limited, and what is applied in practice does not always reflect what has been found in research. Most experts do not suggest that protein needs for active athletes are increased. Essentially athletes will inevitably consume more protein, and will take protein shakes to coincide with the increased demands of resistance training; however, in reality the increased requirement for protein will ultimately be met by the increased energy intake of players via their diet.

Micronutrients

Where macronutrients comprise the majority of the diet, micronutrients have an essential role, and are key in enabling the body to release the energy found in the macronutrients. Micronutrients are also necessary for the formation of hormones, bone, blood and teeth. They are generally grouped into vitamins and minerals.

Vitamins

Vitamins are identified as chemical compounds required to perform special functions in all areas of the body, and are broadly classified as fat soluble and water soluble. Fat-soluble vitamins are stored in the body's tissue, indicating that these do not have to be consumed daily. In contrast water-soluble vitamins are located in the body's fluids, and so a deficiency of these vitamins can quickly prevail, and can be identified significantly more quickly than fat-soluble vitamins. The 'Vitamins' table provides an overview of all the main vitamins alongside the food sources in which these vitamins can be found, and their main function.

There is generally a misconception that people participating in sport should consume vitamin supplements, however there is no scientific research to support this notion. A well balanced diet will provide the body with sufficient amounts of each of the main vitamins to sustain health and performance. However, exceeding the RDA (Recommended Daily Allowance) of vitamins can be detrimental to

Vitamins

Vitamin		Food Sources	Main Function
Water soluble			
B1	Thiamin	Meat, whole grains, legumes, nuts	Involved in the release of energy
B2	Riboflavin	Liver, dairy produce, meat, cereal	Involved in the release of energy
B6	Pyridoxine	Meat, fish, green leafy vegetables, whole grains	Amino acid metabolism
B12	Cyano-cobalamin	Meat, fish, dairy produce	Formation of red blood cells
Niacin		Liver, meat, fish, peanuts cereal products	Nervous system funciton
Folic acid		Liver, legumes, green leafy vegetables	Liver function
C	Ascorbic acid	Green leafy vegetables, fruit, potatoes, white bread	Formation of skin, cartilage, tendon and bone
Fat soluble			
A	Retinol or carotene	Liver, dairy produce, eggs, carrots	Growth and repair of body tissue
D	Calciferols	Dairy produce, action of sunlight	Growth of bone and teeth
E	Tocopherols	Vegetable oils, liver, green leafy vegetables dairy produce, whole grains	New blood vessels around damaged tissue

Minerals

Mineral	Food Sources	Main Function
Sodium	Salt, cheese, muscle/organ meats, fish, bacon	Body fluid volume, nervous system
Potassium	Meat, milk, vegetables, cereals, nuts	Nervous system function, heart rhythm
Calcium	Milk, cheese, nuts, green vegetables, bread	Builds bones and teeth
Magnesium	Green vegetables, meats, dairy produce, cereals	Neuromuscular activity
Phosphorous	Grains and cereals, meat, milk, green vetables	Necessary in metabolism, bones, teeth
Iron	Nuts/seeds, red muscle/organ meats, eggs	Haemoglobin/myoglobin formation
Zinc	Muscle meats, seafood, green vegetables	Enzyme synthesis
Copper	Shellfish, organ meats, nuts, legumes, chocolate	Enzyme synthesis
Iodine	Seafood, eggs, dairy product	Thyroid function
Fluoride	Seafood, water, tea	Tooth structure
Manganese	Nuts, dried fruit, cereals/grains, tea	Enzyme synthesis
Chromium	Meats and dairy products, eggs	Glucose/insulin metabolism
Selenium	Seafood, organ and muscle meats, grains	Anti-oxidant election transfer

health as the body is incapable of dealing with the non-physiological intake of many vitamins, in particular fat-soluble vitamins, without such side effects as headaches, vomiting and kidney damage.

Minerals

Minerals are a very important micronutrient and are essential for structure, function and regulation within the body. Minerals can be classified into major and trace minerals, which coincides with their respective required amounts. Major minerals are required in excess of 100mg, whereas trace minerals are required in amounts of less than 100mg. Like vitamins, sufficient levels of minerals can be consumed in a well balanced diet, therefore additional mineral supplementation is generally not necessary, except in cases where there is a diagnosed deficiency. The 'Minerals' table provides an overview of all the major and trace minerals alongside their main function in the body and food sources in which these vitamins can be found.

Energy

The vast majority of functions performed by cells in the body require energy. Energy is ultimately needed by the body to stay alive, grow, keep warm, as well as to perform physical activity. As we have discussed, energy is derived from the consumption of macronutrients, and this process is aided by the key role of micronutrients. There is no 'magic' food which contains every nutrient the body requires for exercise, therefore an understanding of the precise quality and quantity of which foods to consume can be beneficial. There are various factors that determine the type and amount of nutrients to eat, such as exercise duration and intensity, as well as individual metabolism. The key is to ensure the body is in a positive balance, and in order for this to be achieved, energy intake must equal energy expenditure. In simple terms, the more you exercise, the more your body will require you to eat – however it is what you eat which is the most important factor.

How is Energy Measured?

Essentially energy is measured by the amount of heat created by its complete breakdown in the body. Energy can be measured in either joules (j) or calories (cal), but because people use large amounts of energy, kilojoules (Kj) and kilocalories (Kcal) will be more commonly used. To help put these figures into perspective, one calorie is equivalent to 4.184 joules. Below is a simple conversion to work out the precise quantity, and how to transfer one unit to another:

1 Kilojoule (Kj) = 1,000 joules
1 Megajoule (Mj) = 1,000,000 joules
1 Kilocalorie (Kcal) = 1,000 calories

To convert from one unit to another:
1 Kcal = 4.184 Kj
1 Mj = 239 Kcal

To put this into perspective with regard to nutrients, certain nutrients yield more energy than others, as demonstrated below:

Carbohydrate = 16Kj/3.8Kcal per gram
Fat = 37Kj/9.0Kcal per gram
Protein = 17Kj/4.0Kcal per gram

So it is clear to see that fat yields the most energy per gram – but as previously mentioned, fat can only be metabolized at less than 60 per cent of VO2max, therefore as soccer is performed at higher intensities than this, carbohydrate still remains the predominant energy source.

How Much Energy Intake is Required in Soccer?

It is difficult to estimate this figure for the general population, as the amount of energy intake required will depend on a number of factors, such as intensity of training and competition, quantity of training, and also the posi-

tional differences in soccer. The actual amount of energy needed will vary from person to person, and depends not only on their activity level but also on their basal metabolic rate (BMR). This is the rate at which a person uses energy to maintain the basic functions of the body – thus an adult will use around 4.6Kj (1.1Kcal) every minute, as all body systems require energy even when they are not active and major muscle groups are at rest.

BMR is measured when a person is at complete rest, and has inter-individual variability within a population group and between different groups. For example, young children have a proportionately high BMR for their size due to their rapid growth and development. Men usually have a higher BMR than women since they tend to have more muscle, and older adults usually have a lower BMR than the young since the amount of muscle tends to decrease with age. The BMR accounts on average for about three-quarters of an individual's energy needs. It therefore remains difficult to advocate a set amount of energy intake recommendations, although research has attempted to report generic group estimates. Fig. 65 indicates the estimated average requirements (EAR) for sedentary males and females of varying ages.

Which Nutrients Should Take Priority?

Energy requirements are individual, however it is possible to incorporate some generic recommendations for the soccer player. As previously stipulated, it is not just about consuming enough food to provide adequate energy to equal energy expenditure: it is just as important to ensure that energy is derived from the correct nutrients. Fig. 66 identifies the macronutrient composition of a sedentary person as compared to a soccer player. This demonstrates that in order to maintain health for sedentary living the diet should be composed of 50 per cent carbohydrate, 15

EAR – Mj/day (Kcal/day)

Age	Boys	Girls
4–6 years	7.16 (1715)	6.46 (1545)
7–10 years	8.24 (1970)	7.28 (1740)
11–14 years	9.27 (2220)	7.72 (1845)
15–18 years	11.5 (2755)	8.83 (2110)

Estimate Average Requirements (EAR) for children and adolescents

		EAR	
Men	Weight (kg)	Mj/Day	Kcal/day
19–49	74	10.6	2,550
50–59	74	10.6	2,550
Women			
19–49	60	8.1	1,940
50–59	63	8.0	1,900

Estimate Average Requirements (EAR) for adults male and females

Fig. 65   Estimated average requirements for children and adolescents. (Source: Department of Health (1991) Dietary Reference Values for Food Energy and Nutrients in the United Kingdom HMSO, London)

per cent protein and 35 per cent fat, which would coincide with the EAR outlined in Fig. 65 in relation to age.

When comparing a sedentary person's requirements to that of a soccer player it is evident that their needs differ. A soccer player's carbohydrate intake increases to 60 per cent as this is the main nutrient used to fuel exercise, protein intake stays at 15 per cent, and fat intake is reduced to 25 per cent. This would be a recommended diet to sustain performance throughout the season. However, there are certain exceptions: for example, if training intensity increases, such as during the pre-season or a heavy match schedule, then requirements may be slightly different. Carbohydrate intake would stay at 60 per cent, but protein would be increased to 20 per cent, as this becomes more important in terms of coping with the extra stress, and fat would therefore be reduced to 20 per cent.

Macronutrient Intake Goals

It is often somewhat difficult to quantify nutrient intake recommendations, considering individual variability and the differences in training duration and intensity. For example, a 60 per cent carbohydrate intake recommendation may be perceived as ambiguous and misleading due to inter-individual differences. There are, however, methods to precisely calculate the optimal nutrient intake for each individual, and the following sections will demonstrate how individual carbohydrate and protein needs can be calculated.

Carbohydrate

Carbohydrate intake should contribute to 60 per cent of a soccer player's diet. However, what does this mean for you? There are more accurate ways of working out the amount of carbohydrate required in a diet, with different intake goals for different levels of exercise. The 'Carbohydrate Calculation' table demonstrates the recommended carbohydrate intake in relation to physical activity level. For example, a recreational soccer player weighing 70kg, training and

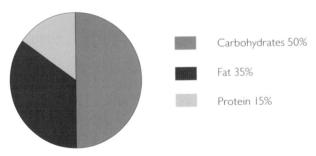

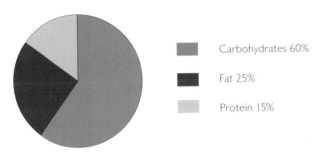

Fig. 66   Nutrient consumption percentage for a soccer player and a sedentary adult.

competing once a week totalling four hours, would calculate their carbohydrate as follows:

Weight in kg × recommended carbohydrate (g) = total intake of carbohydrate necessary (g)
70 × 4 = 280g of carbohydrate required

Therefore to sustain training and competition this person weighing 70kg would need to consume 280g of carbohydrate per day.

The calculated carbohydrate intake goals can be achieved through a variety of foods. The following table identifies a wide range of foods with details of their respective carbohydrate content to help the player structure their carbohydrate intake to ensure they are consuming sufficient amounts to meet the demands of their individual training and competition needs.

Carbohydrate Calculation

Minimal physical exercise	2–3g carbohydrate per kg of body mass
Light physical exercise (3–5 hours per week)	4–5g carbohydrate per kg of body mass
Medium physical exercise (10 hours per week)	6–7g carbohydrate per kg of body mass
Professional/elite athletes (20+ hours per week)	7+g carbohydrate per kg of body mass

Carbohydrate Content

Food	Portion size	Carbohydrate (g) per portion	Kcals per portion
Breakfast cereals			
Cornflakes	1 small bowl (30g)	26	108
Weetabix	2 (40g)	30	141
Grains/pasta			
Couscous	5 tbsp (150g)	77	341
Brown rice	6 tbsp (180g)	58	254
White rice	6 tbsp (180g)	56	248
Spaghetti	4 tbsp (220g) cooked	49	229
Breads			
Bagel	1 (90g)	46	241
White bread	1 large slice (38g)	18	85
Wholemeal bread	1 large slice (38g)	16	82
Pizza	1 large slice (115g)	38	288
Biscuits and cakes			
Digestive	1 (15g)	10	71
Oatmeal	1 (13g)	8	57
Rich Tea	1 (10g)	8	40
Muffin	1 (68g)	34	192
Vegetables			
Boiled new potato	7 small (175g)	27	116
Mashed potato	4 tbsp (180g)	28	188
Sweetcorn	2 tbsp (85g)	17	94
Fruit			
Pineapple	1 slice (80g)	8	33
Raisins	1 tbsp (30g)	21	82
Watermelon	1 slice (200g)	14	62
Dairy products			
Ice cream	1 scoop (60g)	14	62
Custard	2 tbsp (120g)	20	140
Full cream milk	half pint (300ml)	14	198
Skimmed milk	half pint (300ml)	15	99
Yoghurt (low fat fruit)	1 carton (150g)	27	135
Snacks and sweets			
Tortilla/corn chips	1 bag (50g)	30	230
Mars bar	1 standard (65g)	43	287
Muesli bar	1 (33g)	20	154
Milk chocolate	1 bar (54g)	31	281
Pulses			
Chick peas	4 tbsp (140g)	24	168
Red kidney beans	4 tbsp (120g)	20	124
Red lentils	4 tbsp (160g)	28	160

PROTEIN CALCULATION

Sedentary	0.8g protein per kg of body mass
General training programme	1.0g protein per kg of body mass
Athlete undertaking heavy training	1.2–1.6g protein per kg of body mass
Athlete undertaking extreme training	2.0g protein per kg of body mass
Athlete undertaking heavy strength training	1.2–1.7g protein per kg of body mass
Adolescent athlete	2.0g protein per kg of body mass

Protein

Protein is generally used for structural purposes within the body such as muscle growth and repair. Depending on your training status it is recommended that protein contributes to approximately 15–20 per cent. As with carbohydrate, the exact requirements of protein can also be calculated. If we continue with the example of a 70kg person training and competing once a week in a general training programme, their protein requirement would be approximately 1.0g of protein per kg of body mass:

Weight in kg × recommended protein (g) = total intake of protein necessary (g)

Thus 70 × 1 = 70g of protein required to be able to recover fully from training and competition. The table 'Protein Calculation' highlights different protein recommendations for a variety of training programme intensities.

There is generally a misconception that when competing in sport you need to take in lots of extra protein in the form of supplements and protein shakes. However, a well balanced diet containing the correct type and amounts of nutrients will be sufficient to meet the demands of the protein requirements for growth and development. The table 'Protein Food Content' identifies a wide range of foods with details of their precise protein content to give a perspective of the type and amount of foods that should be consumed to ensure

the body is provided with sufficient amounts of protein.

Nutritional Strategies

Coaches and players need to understand nutrition in order to successfully incorporate a nutritional strategy. With an understanding of macronutrients and micronutrients and how they contribute to energy, it is possible to apply this knowledge to be able to enhance performance. We have looked at the quality and quantity of nutrients, and the most relevant source of energy in relation to soccer – however, it is just as imperative to understand when we need to consume these particular foods to gain the most benefit for match days and performance.

The Timing of Nutrient Intake

Carbohydrate has been identified as the predominant nutrient for energy when playing soccer due to the high intensity, intermittent nature of the sport. It is therefore recommended that 60 per cent of the diet should be comprised of carbohydrates. It is evident from the table 'Carbohydrate Content' that a vast number of foods contain carbohydrate, so which exact food containing carbohydrate is most appropriate? As previously discussed, carbohydrate comes in different forms and can generally be grouped into simple and complex carbohydrates. The body requires

Protein Food Content

Food	Protein (g/portion)
MEAT/FISH/POULTRY	
Red meat (4oz portion)	32
Chicken (6oz portion)	38
White fish (6oz portion)	30
Oily fish (6oz portion)	30
Sausages (2)	15
Mince (4oz)	25
Tinned tuna (4oz)	25
DAIRY PRODUCTS AND EGGS	
Milk ½ pint)	10
Cottage cheese (4oz)	15
Fromage frais (4oz)	8
Cheddar cheese (2oz)	14
Yoghurt (1 carton)	8
Eggs (2)	14
PULSES AND NUTS	
Kidney beans (8oz boiled)	15
Baked beans (½ large tin)	10
Lentils (8oz boiled)	15
Nuts (2oz)	13
CEREALS	
Bread (2 slices)	6
Pasta (6oz boiled)	5
Rice (6oz boiled)	4
OTHER	
Tofu	9

these different types of carbohydrate at different times in order to optimize performance.

The glycaemic index (GI) refers to the rate at which carbohydrate is absorbed into the blood as glucose and is therefore available to the muscle, to be used as energy or stored as glycogen. Carbohydrates that break down quickly during digestion and release glucose rapidly into the bloodstream have a high GI; those that break down more slowly, releasing glucose more gradually into the bloodstream, have a low GI and are subsequently rated on a continuum of 1–100. Therefore foods with a high GI rating are useful for refuelling and enhancing recovery or for providing energy during exercise, whereas those foods with a moderate to low GI rating are useful for pre-competition meals, due to their slower, sustained release of energy.

Fig. 67 demonstrates the difference in

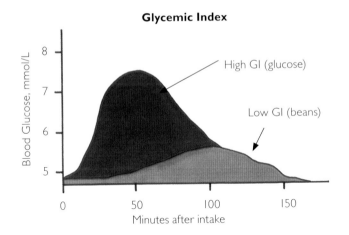

Glycemic Index

Fig. 67 Graph highlighting the differences in energy release and duration in high and low GI foods.

energy release from high and low GI foods, and also the duration of energy release. If you observe the graph you can see high GI foods increase blood glucose to higher levels compared to low GI foods, but the increase is short-lived, whereas although low GI foods do not increase blood glucose to such high levels they do allow for the sustained release of CHO for a prolonged period.

Care must also be taken with the ingestion of rapidly absorbed carbohydrate prior to training or match days, as these must be specifically timed to gain the maximum benefit. When glucose enters the bloodstream the body produces a hormone called insulin. Insulin has the job of removing excess glucose in order to keep the body's blood sugar levels constant. However, consuming high GI foods close to the onset of exercise (approximately 15–20 minutes before) prevents the production of insulin, allowing the circulating glucose to remain available for energy. On the other hand, consuming high GI foods more than thirty minutes from the start of training/the match, and the insulin produced will not only prevent the carbohydrate (glucose) being used as an energy source, it will also reduce the body's ability to use fat for energy. Ultimately this means that your muscles have

no readily available energy supplies, causing an even faster depletion of those limited glycogen stores, resulting in fatigue and poor performance.

The 'Glycemic Index Rating' table highlights some examples of carbohydrate foods along with their GI rating to identify the most appropriate foods to consume at the correct time.

Pre-Match Strategies

Pre-match nutritional strategies attempt to achieve a number of goals. As we have discussed, carbohydrate in the form of glycogen is the most important energy source for soccer, and there is only limited capacity for storage. It is therefore essential that the athlete consumes the right food to keep these stores topped up, to ensure there is enough glycogen to fuel the exercise. Furthermore it is crucial to restore liver glycogen content. This is an especially important factor when the training/match takes place in the morning, as liver glycogen content will be reduced following sleep, as no food will have been consumed during this time – an overnight fast can result in liver glycogen being reduced to less than 20g. It is also important that while the athlete should avoid feeling hungry, equally

Glycaemic Index Rating of Various Foods

Food item	GI	Food item	GI	Food item	GI
Baked potatoes	83	Pineapple	61	Peas	48
Rice cakes	82	Ice cream	61	Orange	43
Rice Krispies	82	Oatmeal	57	Apple juice	41
Graham crackers	74	Orange juice	55	Spaghetti (white)	41
Mashed potatoes	73	Popcorn	55	Spaghetti (wholemeal)	37
Bagel	72	Oatmeal biscuits	55	Apple	36
Carrots	71	White/brown rice	55	Sweetened yoghurt	33
White bread	70	Sweet potatoes	54	Skimmed milk	32
Wholewheat bread	69	Banana	53	Soya beans	18
Shredded wheat	69	Baked beans	48	Peanuts	14
Soft drinks	68				

he should avoid causing any gastrointestinal upset. Current advice is that to avoid such stomach upsets, the player trials whatever he intends to consume before it is incorporated into the match day's preparation.

Finally, good hydration is essential. Dehydration of 2 per cent of a player's bodyweight can lead to reductions in performance (fluid and hydration will be covered later in the chapter).

The timing of an athlete's pre-event strategy is crucial to ensure that the right nutrients are available at the right time. As a general guideline the pre-event meal should be consumed two to four hours before, because during this time carbohydrate is metabolized into muscle glycogen; however, timing may differ, depending on an individual's metabolism. This timing should be seen as a guideline only, because it is imperative to account for individual tolerance in terms of what and when people can eat before a match, taking into consideration the kick-off time. For example, if training or a match takes place in the morning, do you get up four hours earlier to consume the pre-event meal, but this would reduce sleeping time and could adversely affect performance, or do you settle for an adequate amount of sleep and then concentrate on ensuring that you have a light snack or meal before the match, and take advantage of opportunities to consume carbohydrate during or at half time?

Essentially pre-match preparation should concentrate on low to moderate GI foods two to four hours prior to exercise, avoiding sugary foods. This should be followed by high GI foods twenty minutes prior to the match or training, although players need to establish their own tolerance for these types of carbohydrate. The following information outlines a pre-match checklist, with ideas for meals and snacks.

The Day Before Competition

It is important to ensure that players:

- Eat and drink regularly throughout the day

- Eat plenty of low GI carbohydrate foods with each meal and snack, such as bread/toast, potatoes, pasta, rice, cereals, fruit (fresh or dried)
- Include a drink with every meal and snack, such as water, fruit juice, squash, cordials and sports drinks; intake of tea and coffee should be limited
- Eat a substantial evening meal with a large portion of low to moderate GI carbohydrates, and a moderate portion of protein such as meat, fish, chicken, cheese or eggs; in addition add plenty of fruit and vegetables
- Drink plenty

Competition Day, Morning Match

If the match is in the morning ensure that players:

- Eat breakfast – choose cereals, toast and fruit juice; for a low fat, cooked alternative, try scrambled/poached eggs on several slices of toast, or a lean, grilled bacon sandwich
- If unable to eat a large breakfast, try a snack such as:
  - Toasted teacake with jam/honey
  - Low fat fruit yoghurt and a banana
  - Low fat rice dessert and two cereal bars
  - Sports bar and a fruit scone with jam
  - Fruit smoothie: blend together some low fat milk and yoghurt, a banana and a teaspoon of honey
- Drink plenty

Competition Day, Afternoon Match

It is important that players eat a pre-competition meal two to four hours before the event; they should choose foods that are low to moderate GI carbohydrates, and low in fat, and should try to establish a routine so they know what competition meal/snack

they are comfortable with. Here are a few suggestions:

- Baked potato with tuna and beans
- Pasta/rice with a low fat tomato sauce
- Chicken with pasta and mushroom sauce
- Breakfast cereals
- Toast with jam/honey/marmalade
- Sandwiches with lean ham, cheese and tomato, chicken salad, tuna and cucumber, cottage cheese
- Low fat yoghurts/rice desserts

Players should also keep well hydrated by drinking plenty.

Post-Match Recovery Strategy

The consumption of nutrients after training and matches is just as important as the pre-match intake. It is imperative to consume the correct nutrients after exercise because you are essentially preparing your body for the next training session or match. The aims of the recovery strategy are to:

- Maximize the rate of glycogen resynthesis to restore depleted liver and muscle glycogen stores
- Replace fluid and electrolytes lost through sweating during exercise
- Consume proteins to regenerate, repair and adapt, following the catabolic stress and damage caused during exercise

The timing and type of nutrients consumed are also very important. In order to recover effectively it is vital to eat and drink immediately after exercise, even if you are not hungry or thirsty, because hunger and thirst – or the lack of them – are not good indicators of what the body requires at this time. There is a window of opportunity during the first two hours following exercise when the highest sustained rates of glycogen storage

Fig. 68 Glycogen resynthesis following exercise.

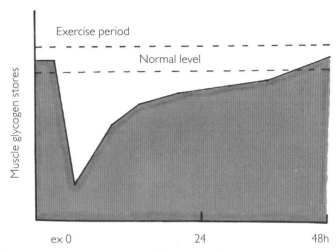

Changes in muscle glycogen stores following exercise. Note that complete repletion takes 24–48 hours.

Source: Nutrition for Sport *by Steve Wootton*

are experienced; after two hours this process becomes significantly slower. Fig. 68 demonstrates the accelerated increase in glycogen resynthesis, followed by a more steady and gradual increase to become fully resynthesized.

It is recommended that players consume 50–100g of high GI carbohydrate within the first twenty minutes post exercise, along with l0g of protein. Then following the immediate consumption of nutrients, a further meal should be consumed approximately two hours post exercise, comprising both complex and simple carbohydrates, moderate protein, and low amounts of fat. The table 'Recovery Foods' highlights potential recovery foods, with their respective nutritional content.

Tips for the Travelling Athlete

Competing in soccer through a whole season can involve a great deal of travel, especially for those playing in a regional or national league. Because of this, it is not always feasible for an athlete to plan, prepare and consume their food two to four hours before kick-off, or they might not have access to the facilities to consume an adequate meal post match. Therefore when travelling to a competition, players need to pack some appropriate food items and drinks so they start the event fully prepared. Similarly, recovery nutrition should start straight after the event, and continue on the way home. The choice of food items will depend on the length of the journey and personal preference. However, a few basic rules apply to all athletes:

- *Schedule* the pre-event meal two to four hours before the start. This allows enough time for foods to be digested
- *Never* try anything new before a competition
- *Avoid* spicy foods or those with a high fat content
- *Include* plenty of carbohydrate foods and moderate amounts of protein foods

Recovery Foods

Average Food Portion	Energy Kcals	Carbohydrate g	Protein g	Fat g
75g/ 4 handfuls raisins	172	50	1	—
Banana, 1 large	63	15	1	0.3
Apple	42	11	0.2	—
Fruit salad in syrup, 130g	124	33	0.5	—
Baked potato × 1	147	35	3.6	—
Pitta bread, 1 wholemeal	159	35	6	1
Bread, wholemeal: medium slice / large loaf: 2 slices	151	28	6	2
1 white bap	147	28	5	2
Malt loaf: 2 slices	161	34	5	1
Chelsea bun × 1	256	40	6	10
Hot cross bun × 1	202	38	5	5
Muesli, no added sugar, 95g serving	348	64	10	8
Weetabix × 2	142	31	4	1
Jaffa cake × 2	73	14	1	2
Muffin, plain	200	35	7	4
Madeira cake, 1 slice	98	15	1	4
Flapjack × 1	145	18	1	8
Jam tart × 1	129	22	1	5
Digestives × 2	141	21	2	6
Wholemeal crackers × 3	92	14	2	3
Oatcakes × 2	115	16	3	5
Pancakes × 2	174	17	5	10
Jelly, 135g	82	20	2	—
Low fat fruit yoghurt, 1 small pot skimmed milk skimmed milk × 1 glass, or 1/3 pint	135	27	6	1
Soya milk × 1glass, or 1/3 pint	64	10	6	0.2
Low fat rice pudding, 1 serving 85g	97	17	3	0.2
Spaghetti boiled, white, 150g	156	33	5	1
Spaghetti canned in tomato sauce, 125g	80	18	3	0.5
Chicken, light meat, 85g	121	—	23	4
Cashew nuts × 20	224	11	7	18
Hard-boiled egg × 1	88	—	8	7
Tuna in oil, drained, 95g	275	—	22	21
Milk chocolate × 150g bar	265	30	4	15
Baked beans, 200g	128	21	10	1

Here are a few ideas for some 'kit-bag' snacks:

- Two slices of malt loaf and a low fat fruit yoghurt
- A white bap filled with tuna and salad, and one large banana
- Four handfuls of raisins and two large handfuls of cashew nuts
- Four oatcakes and a glass of low fat milk
- A small can of rice pudding and a Chelsea bun
- A small can of fruit salad in syrup, two plain digestives, an apple and a hard-boiled egg
- Flapjack, a carton of soya milk and a plain muffin
- Two pancakes and a hot cross bun
- One large pitta bread filled with one chicken portion, with salad and two Jaffa cakes
- Pasta salad with tuna and a small chocolate bar
- Two jam tarts and a hard-boiled egg
- Two Weetabix with skimmed milk and a chopped banana

When travelling, always pack more than you think you might eat, as you never know when you might be delayed. Ensure that appropriate types of food are eaten both before and after the event, though be sure to avoid overeating before the event. In order to enhance recovery rate after the competition, start eating and drinking as soon as possible: remember the twenty-minute window of opportunity to accelerate glycogen resynthesis immediately after exercise. Where possible, try to vary the foods that you take with you, and remember to pack plenty of fluids in order to promote rehydration.

Helpful Hints

There is a misconception that you have to be an experienced chef to cook and eat healthily. This is not the case, however, although for those who are not sure how to cook certain foods, then cookery books can provide a step-by-step guide. Also, food does not always have to be hot for it to be nutritious. Foods such as cereals and sandwiches can be great alternatives for those who have not got the time or facilities to prepare hot food. Keep cupboards stocked with a selection of cold meats, low fat cheese, tinned fish and nut butters, which make quick and nutritious fillings for sandwiches. For those who prefer to consume cereals, try including chopped fresh and dried fruit, nuts and mixed seeds to increase the nutritional value.

Athletes can be deterred from consuming the correct nutrients due to time constraints, especially post training when they are feeling fatigued. One solution may be to make a large pan of pasta, and once it has cooled, drizzle it with a little olive oil and store in a sealed container in the fridge. This pasta can be mixed with various sauces and mixed vegetables over the next few days for a quick meal or snack. Some athletes often face the dilemma that they know they need to be consuming the correct nutrients, but they don't feel hungry first thing in the morning or immediately after training or competition.

For those who feel adventurous, one option could be to make high energy smoothies. Here are a couple of recipes:

Banana and Honey Smoothie
300ml skimmed milk
150g/one small pot of low fat, fruit yoghurt
One ripe banana
1–2 teaspoons honey

Blend all the ingredients until a smooth consistency is reached. Once this is achieved, serve immediately, or keep refrigerated, or keep in a flask. This one glass of smoothie will equate to approximately 444Kcal, providing 95g carbohydrate, 17g protein and 1.7g fat.

Raspberry and Orange Smoothie
250g raspberries
200ml natural (plain) yogurt
300ml freshly squeezed orange juice

Place the raspberries and yoghurt in a food processor or blender, and process for about 1min until smooth and creamy. Then add the orange juice to the raspberry and yoghurt mixture and process for about 30sec, or until thoroughly combined. Pour into tall glasses and serve immediately. This portion will serve approximately three to four people. One glass will equate to approximately 170Kcal, providing 33g carbohydrate, 9g protein and 1.3g fat.

These are suggestions for a relatively simple way of gaining a high energy intake from a home-made drink if you find it difficult to consume foods immediately post training and competition, or first thing if you have a morning event.

Fluid and Hydration

Macronutrients and micronutrients have been discussed with regard to their importance to energy for exercise. However, hydration status before and during exercise is equally important to optimize soccer performance. Water is approximately 50–70 per cent of the total body mass, the precise amount depending on the individual body composition, considering that 70 per cent of the mass of muscle is water, in comparison to only 10 per cent of fat mass attributed to water.

Water is crucial to the body as it has very important roles: as the largest component of blood it is vital in transporting substances throughout the body; it is also vital to the transfer of gases in the lungs; and it acts as a lubricant in joints, heart, lungs and eyes. In addition water plays a role in the body's thermoregulation, particularly during exercise, absorbing the heat generated from energy and relocating it to the skin's surface for eventual dissipation. Water is excreted as sweat, which has a cooling effect when evaporating from the body. This can be problematic however, because essential electrolytes, and in particular sodium, is lost via sweating, which can be detrimental to performance. This can be especially challenging in soccer as sweat sodium losses can be greater in high intensity sports, ranging from 1.7 to 7g of salt lost in 100min of soccer training.

Monitoring Fluid Loss

Contrary to popular belief, thirst is not a good indication of dehydration. Thirst mechanisms underestimate actual fluid requirements, which result in involuntary dehydration, due to simply not thinking you need to be drinking fluid. This can have detrimental effects, because even as little as 2–3 per cent loss of water in relation to body mass can seriously impair performance. Dehydration may result in a number of negative side effects, such as a decrease in muscle strength, speed, stamina, energy and cognitive skills, as well as an increase in the risk of injury and perceived effort of exertion, all of which are essential to optimizing soccer performance.

To monitor the amount of fluid lost after exercise you can weigh yourself (nude) pre and post training or match, where each gram of weight lost equates to one millilitre of fluid lost. For example, one kilogram of weight lost would equate to one litre of fluid lost, which would indicate the amount of fluid necessary to rehydrate yourself. Another method by which to monitor hydration status is to observe the colour of your urine (Fig. 69), which should be a clear straw-like colour when euhydrated (when the body water is in balance).

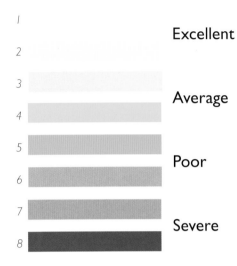

Fig. 69   Urine chart to monitor hydration levels via the colour of the urine.

Hydration Strategies

The consumption of fluid is the key to maintaining euhydration, but it is also an effective strategy by which to gain additional energy to sustain performance during training and matches. Sports drinks can be very effective, containing the carbohydrates and electrolytes necessary for performance. As previously mentioned, sweating results in the loss of electrolytes and sodium, which is a major factor causing cramping. Therefore the ingestion of sports drinks can replace lost sodium and electrolytes and delay the onset of fatigue. Sports drinks are also effective for immediate recovery as they contain high GI carbohydrates, and are therefore ideal for the quick consumption of carbohydrate to start the refuelling process.

It is important to note that there are also issues to be aware of with sports drinks. Due to the added carbohydrate and sodium in sports drinks, water uptake and retention is greater in comparison to water. However, if the amount of carbohydrate is too great then water uptake is decreased and thus hydration is not achieved. It is therefore recommended that you should only consume a sports drink that has less than 8 per cent of carbohydrate. Furthermore, due to the high GI content of sport drinks they can also be detrimental to your teeth when taken in excessive amounts, or over a prolonged period.

When considering a hydration strategy, and in particular fluid intake, a number of factors should be considered:

- Begin exercise well hydrated
- Develop a fluid intake plan for during matches
- Examine your sport to identify opportunities for fluid intake
- Cool, palatable drinks are recommended, to promote and encourage fluid intake
- Water is adequate to replace fluid losses, but additional benefits are apparent from drinking carbohydrate-electrolyte drinks (sports drinks), during long, intense matches
- Develop good drinking practices during training, and integrate these strategies during matches
- Undertake active rehydration and refuelling strategies after long, intense matches, as the replacement of sodium is important

Can Alcohol be used to Rehydrate after Exercise?

It is not uncommon for most amateur or semi-professional teams to consume alcohol in the club house after a match, as well as some professional footballers, who have openly admitted to alcohol addiction. During a soccer match players will lose a considerable amount of fluid, which will need to be replaced, therefore can alcohol be used to replace such fluid? The answer to this is, quite frankly, no. Alcohol is a diuretic, like caffeine, which means that it draws water out of the body and promotes dehydration, thus having completely the opposite effect to what the body requires post exercise.

Alcohol also contains many calories and few nutrients, and is therefore of no benefit or help in the replenishment of glycogen. Like most empty calories, those from alcohol are stored as fat and will actually cause the body to burn less fat. In addition, alcohol inhibits the absorption of vitamins and minerals from our food, and promotes their excretion. Therefore, if we consider that there is an optimal window of two hours in which there is an opportunity to accelerate glycogen resynthesis immediately after exercise, consuming alcohol post exercise can actually interfere with glycogen repletion, thereby delaying recovery.

Obviously, therefore, there is no place for alcohol in the diet of athletes, because in addition to the issues of resynthesizing glycogen, the excessive consumption of alcohol also has adverse effects on health, affecting cardiac and skeletal muscle and the liver in particular. It is worth noting, too, that in the past, alcohol consumption has been associated with the shortening of the career of a number of professional footballers.

INDEX